TO MAGGIE, WITH LOVE.
WE WILL GET THERE
SOME DAY.
LOVE. PAT
1999

D1199968

# LOST LHASA

*With the Potala in the
background, government
ministers ride horses led
by red-hatted servants.*

*The Western Gate and the Potala*

# LOST LHASA

## Heinrich Harrer's Tibet

Text and photographs by Heinrich Harrer

Harry N. Abrams, Inc., Publishers, New York

## Acknowledgments

*I would like to thank the following individuals who have helped me with this book:*
*Samuel Antupit, Leslie DiRusso, Adele Hammond, John Harlin, Carina Harrer,*
*Judith Henry, Julia Moore, Bill Phillips, Hugh Edward Richardson, Steve Roper,*
*David Swanson, Jigme Taring, Rinchen Drölma Taring,*
*Rakra Rinpoche (T.C. Tethong), and Dadul Namgyel Tsarong (George)*

PROJECT MANAGER: JULIA MOORE

EDITOR: JOHN HARLIN III
DESIGNER: ADELE HAMMOND

Library of Congress Cataloging-in-Publication Data
Harrer, Heinrich, 1912–
Lost Lhasa: Heinrich Harrer's Tibet / text and photographs by Heinrich Harrer;
introduction by Galen Rowell.
p.   cm.
Includes bibliographical references and index.
ISBN 0–8109–3560–0 (cloth)/ISBN 0–8109–2789–6 (pbk.)
I. Lhasa (China)—Social life and customs. I. Title.
DS796.L46H37 1992
951' .5—dc20                                               92–7211

Text and photographs copyright © 1992 Heinrich Harrer
Introduction copyright © 1992 Galen Rowell
Map copyright © 1992 Summit Publications, Incorporated. Cartography by
Matthew Kania; adapted from original work by Heinrich Harrer and Zasak J. Taring
Chapter head drawings of Tibetan lucky signs copyright © 1992 Phunstock Dorje

Paperback edition published in 1997 by Harry N. Abrams, Incorporated, New York
All rights reserved. No part of the contents of this book may be reproduced
without the written permission of the publisher
Produced by Summit Publications, Incorporated, Hood River. Oregon

Clothbound edition published in 1992 by Harry N. Abrams, Inc.

Printed and bound in the United States of America

Harry N. Abrams, Inc.
100 Fifth Avenue
New York, N.Y. 10011
www.abramsbooks.com

*For the children of Tibet*

*Giant* thangkas *on the Potala*

# CONTENTS

*In part to combat the influence of*
*gambling, I introduced the blanket toss and*
*several other sports to Tibet.*

# PREFACE

*Heinrich Harrer*

Soon after he received the Nobel Peace Prize in 1989, His Holiness the Dalai Lama declared 1991 as "The Year of Tibet." Four decades had passed since the Chinese invasion of Tibet in 1950. Three decades had passed since the Dalai Lama's sad flight from his homeland. For much of this time, Tibet slipped from being the "Forbidden Country" of legend to being the "Forgotten Country." With his declaration, the Dalai Lama intended to rouse the world's attention to the Tibetan cause. Comfortably ensconced in my home in Liechtenstein, I heard the call. My response is this book.

Locked in my drawers lay several thousand photographic negatives of Tibet from before the Chinese invasion; most had never been published. So I made prints from the negatives, and with a suitcase full of a thousand precious pictures, I took off for India. There I visited old Tibetan friends who had lived with me in Lhasa during the 1940s, when it was still the capital of a free country. In Rajpur, India, I met the great old gentleman Jigme Taring and his charming wife Rinchen Drölma. Both have published excellent books on Tibet, and I think they have unsurpassed knowledge of their lost homeland. In Kalimpong I met Dadul Namgyel Tsarong, better known as George, one of the few Tibetan officers who had risked taking pictures himself.

Showing my friends these photographs had an incredible effect. Immediately I was surrounded by three generations of Tibetans and in no time my neatly organized bundles were chaos. Monks from the nearby monastery joined our group, children and servants showed up, and the world around us was forgotten. Relatives were pointed out with shouts of joy, but quiet tears fell when the Tibetans recognized fathers or brothers who had lost their lives opposing the Chinese. Even so, the pictures brought back happy thoughts and memories of a relatively carefree time in a Tibet that is no longer.

Moved by this enthusiasm, I went on to Dharamsala, India, to show the pictures to the Dalai Lama. With his blessing, I was finally poised to fulfill my long-held dream of a photo book that would show Tibet the way it was and be a testament to the high standard of its old culture.

So much has been lost since my unforgettable five years in the city. To Western eyes, this was a strange place full of the inexplicable and the occult. Tibet was, and still is, a country with a people who respect nature and mystery, who believe in a god-king, magic, and spiritual adventure. Perhaps more than ever, Tibetan culture and religion fascinate the world.

The Tibetans' profound faith in old manners and customs made it extraordinarily difficult to photograph festivals, processions, and high officers during their intimate rituals. Their love for old customs was deeply anchored and deserved respect. As I had become a trusted government employee, I took pains not to hurt the feelings of the Tibetans. And it was probably my esteem and love for these hospitable people that allowed me eventual acceptance into their society. Although I risked offending their sense of privacy, I felt it important to document Tibetan culture, and this book is the fruit of my discreet labor.

My journey to Lhasa with Peter Aufschnaiter took two years, during which time we lived and worked with farmers in the south, staying in their homes, eating their food. We took shelter in the warm tents of nomads in the north, bartered with traders and caravan guides, and finally arrived in Lhasa, starved and nearly penniless. At all times, even during the extremely cold winter months we had made drawings, kept diaries, and learned to read and write Tibetan. In the capital we soon realized that this society, medieval and feudal though it was, showed great wisdom and intelligence. We often found that our pride and conceit in Western achievements were inappropriate.

It's with an eye to the richness of the past and the potential of Tibetans left to themselves that I offer this book. Other literature—even my own previous books—provides geographical information, adventure stories, and exquisite photography. But little presents a view of the past, especially the daily life in the "Forbidden City."

With their deep faith, the Tibetans have survived incredible sufferings. They continue to be indestructible and united in their sense of nationhood. In this spirit, I dedicate this book to the children of Tibet, with the hope that they never forget their origins. Whatever fate decides for Tibetans, their snow-covered mountains, the throne of their gods, will stand unchanged. Unchanged also are the flights of wild geese and black-necked cranes in the cold, moonlit nights over Lhasa. Their wingbeat make a sound like Lha Gye Lo: The gods shall prevail!

Memories make me happy, for only nice things stay clear; therefore the work on this book has given me great pleasure. I do hope that the Tibetans and their friends will also find pleasure and happiness in these pages.

*School days, Lhasa*

*Pilgrim on the Lingkor, below Chagpori*

# MESSAGE

Heinrich Harrer and I first met because he and my elder brother, Lobsang Samten, had become good friends and even got up to mischief together. Eventually I asked him to come and see me on the pretext that he could help me work on the generator for my movie projector. We too soon became friends. Now, as we both grow older, we remember those happy days we spent together in a happy country. It is a sign of genuine friendship that it doesn't change, come what may—once you get to know each other, you retain your friendship and help each other for the rest of your lives. Harrer has always been such a friend to Tibet. His most important contribution to our cause was his book, *Seven Years in Tibet*, which introduced hundreds of thousands of people to my country. Still today, he is active in the struggle for Tibetan people's freedoms and rights, and we are grateful to him for it.

*Tenzin Gyatso*
*The Fourteenth Dalai Lama*

*Chinese pagodas and Chagpori, atop which sits the medical school*

# INTRODUCTION

*Galen Rowell*

The legend about Heinrich Harrer arriving in Lhasa as a prison-camp escapee in the disguise of a Tibetan nomad is not entirely true. After escaping, he spent two years trying to reach Lhasa; but despite his intense blue eyes and matted blond beard, he wore no disguises during the journey. By the time he arrived in Lhasa, he had essentially adopted the lifestyle of a Tibetan nomad.

When World War II broke out, Harrer was on a mountaineering expedition in India. Because he was an Austrian citizen, the British placed him in an internment camp. After their escape, he and his Austrian climbing partner, Peter Aufschnaiter, were immersed in the culture of Tibet as deeply as any Westerners in history. They lived with the local people and traveled like nomads as they made their way across high plains and passes. Their goal was not to tour, document, or plunder Tibet, but to escape the persecution and stress of a world in chaos in the way they knew best: to head for the mountains.

In adventure movies we are used to seeing disguises come off to reveal our hero with a superweapon. But as Harrer and Aufschnaiter entered Lhasa on an icy January day in 1946, their tattered sheepskin cloaks hid only starved and blistered bodies. They had lived off the land by a combination of ingenuity, stealth, and the natural generosity of the Tibetan people. They arrived in Lhasa with no money, no weapons, and no cameras or film. But they had learned to speak the language, and they were thinking about staying for the rest of their lives. In the best tradition of a Tibetan pilgrimage, they had undertaken a difficult journey to a holy place with few possessions and no promise of external reward. Because they were not required to proceed and their motivation came from their hearts, Lhasa had become their Nirvana. The attitudes of the other pilgrims they met in the frozen highlands paralleled Harrer's own as he had approached the mountains of Europe: voluntarily confronting adversity for the intense feeling of liberation of the spirit that comes with the experience.

They were also moved by the frequent sight of wildlife at close range, much of it found nowhere else in the world. "When we traveled through the westernmost part of Tibet, the *drong* [wild yaks] and *kiang* [wild asses] accompanied us all the time. The kiang were curious and unafraid. And then there were the *nawa* [Tibetan blue sheep], the *nyan* [great argali sheep], the *gowa* [gazelle] and the *chiru* [antelope]. The hoofed animals were always in herds and were part of our everyday life. The *kiang* were always interested to see us. They would come look and then suddenly the stallion would give the order and take them all off. Then they are standing there again along your route, watching you."

In October 1950, nearly five years after Harrer and Aufschnaiter reached Lhasa, the Peoples Liberation Army of Communist China marched into the interior of Tibet. If it had been an isolated act of Communist aggression, the free world might have focused on it, but clouds of political change had been sweeping the Asian continent for the past year. The United States had just gone to war against Communism in Korea—a battle that engaged the Chinese—and chose not to assist Tibet in its resistance to Communist China. On January 20, 1951, an Associated Press story about Tibet hinted at the presence of the two Austrians alongside the Dalai Lama during his escape from Lhasa: "The flight of the young Dalai Lama from his capital in Communist-invaded Tibet was one of the strangest journeys ever made by a monarch. [An] aide and two European technicians, who accompanied the Dalai Lama, said the Red Chinese flag already was flying over the old Chinese residency in Lhasa, the capital, when plans . . . for the Dalai Lama's dramatic trip over a perilous icy trail were made in utmost secrecy. . . . Stars glowed with winter brilliance as the Dalai Lama made his way from the palace alone about 2:00 A.M. the next morning. . . . Ten miles from Lhasa the boy king descended from the palanquin (covered chair) and gazed back at the white mass of the Potala Palace lighted by the first rays of the morning sun. . . . It was apparent from questions he asked that he was uncertain where his travels would end."

After Harrer returned to war-torn Europe, he lay awake, homesick for Tibet. He settled in neutral Liechtenstein and sat down to finish *Seven Years in Tibet*, which was published in 1953. In Tibet he had kept a detailed personal diary, and even as he was fleeing he began work on his book. One reason he wrote his story, instead of immediately assembling his photographs into a more visual book, which would also have sold, was American journalist Lowell Thomas's parting remark at the end of a brief visit to Lhasa in 1949: "If you don't do your biography soon, I will."

The book was an instant bestseller, translated into forty-eight languages. In parts of the world Harrer's incredible tale of adventure and courage sold second only to the Bible. (It was the first of two dozen works by Harrer on mountains, adventures, and cultures around the world.) He became a celebrity overnight, and the 3,000-odd negatives and slides he had carried across the Himalaya took on a significance for him quite different from his original intention for them. They served as validation of the verbal account of his adventure, rather than wordless memories to contemplate or share with his Tibetan friends. In the forty years since he left Tibet, Harrer has published only a handful of those pictures, until now, with the publication of *Lost Lhasa.*

On the whole, Harrer photographed Lhasa and Lhasans in order to have a visual diary, rather than to titilate the public for commercial gain as was so common among other photographers of the period who documented exotic cultures. The sensitivity of his "style" was ahead of its time, coming long before it became fashionable for photographers to immerse themselves in a culture to show its inner values. Harrer made no effort to focus on unusual customs with an eye for the attention they would grab from the folks back home. He *was* at home. The implied comparison of "us" and "them" in order to exploit the strangeness of Tibet is not part of his work because, as he explains, "I tried to behave like a Tibetan. I avoided trying to make close-ups of the Dalai Lama, because no Tibetan would think of doing that." This attitude sets Harrer's images far apart from pictures made by the few other Western photographers who spent time in Tibet before 1950.

Only during his last days, when rumors of the Chinese invasion reached Lhasa, did he set out to photograph with what could be called documentary intentions. "I knew it would be a long time before I saw Lhasa again, so I bade farewell to all the places I had come to love. One day I rode out with my camera and took as many photos as I could, feeling that they would revive happy memories in the future and perhaps win the sympathy of others for this beautiful and strange land."

Harrer's inhibitions about photographing the Dalai Lama lessened as he fled Tibet to a border town in the Chumbi Valley, where he again spent a few months with the young ruler, knowing that he might never see him again. Harrer's main coverage of Tibet had been in black and white, but he had saved a few frames from his only two rolls of color film, which Lowell Thomas had given him. The fact that Harrer's last photograph of the Dalai Lama in Tibet became the first color cover of *Life* magazine is less coincidental than it sounds. Not many covers for the magazine came from amateurs, but in those final days Harrer had begun to think journalistically.

Harrer's principal camera, a 35mm Leica, was bartered from a Tibetan noble who brought it from India. His black-and-white film came from a hundred-meter roll of 35mm motion picture stock that had been left in Lhasa by an earlier expedition and preserved by the cold, dry climate. He cut it into rolls for the Leica and processed it in Lhasa with the help of a Mohammedan trader who did some portraits for people there. "When we looked into the chemicals, out came the shadows of the dark clouds and the white buildings [of a test roll shot of the Potala Palace] ... you can't imagine how happy I was!" Occasionally he borrowed a bigger, medium-format camera, for which both film and developing had to be procured in India—with a long delay for the two crossings of the Himalaya—but most of the work that appears in this book came from the Leica and the hundred-meter roll of movie film found in Lhasa.

After he returned to Europe and processed his few color slides, "no one would believe the colors—the film, everyone said, must be faulty and the colors not true: no sky could be that blue, no water could sparkle that green." Harrer knew otherwise. His eyes had seen a similar world with "these incredibly intense colors, that hard azure-blue, that eye-calming green of the grass," which his excellent exposures brought out. The fact that he knew this saturated color would be absent from his black-and-white work may have influenced how much his Tibetan coverage focuses on the culture, rather than on the natural mountain landscape that was so dear to him.

In Tibet, Harrer was not in a position to be an innovator in photography. He had his hands full just trying to make his images come out. We can be thankful for this, because photographs by amateurs whose intentions are simple and direct, as Harrer's were, often end up being far better documents of vanishing cultures than the work of professionals with artistic or commercial motives. The record of the American Old West, as an example, is far more truthfully and powerfully revealed in albums of family snapshots than in more technically perfect images of people in their Sunday finest posed against contrived backgrounds by professionals. Harrer's Tibet imagery has the integrity of a family album, but with great attention to particulars.

Harrer's approach to photography reflects the same dedication to detail and excellence that is the hallmark of all his chosen pursuits. He learned the radically new technique of parallel skiing well enough to compete in the 1936 Winter Olympics. Harrer's 1938 first ascent of the north face of the Eiger in Switzerland was long considered the most difficult climb in history. Before Harrer's ascent, eight out of ten climbers had died during their own attempts on the face. He made the climb with the clear intention that it would be a stepping-stone to the Himalaya. He wanted to be chosen for an expedition because otherwise "to get to the Himalayas one had either to be very rich or to belong to the nation whose sons at that time still had the chance of being sent to India on service. For a man who was neither British nor wealthy there was only one way . . . do something which made it impossible for one's claims to be passed over."

Harrer lived in Lhasa for two years before he met and befriended the Dalai Lama. Following custom, the Dalai Lama was kept sequestered from all but his spiritual and political advisors. As the spiritual and temporal ruler of his people, the teenager was unable to walk the streets of Lhasa. His passage through town was always prepared in advance and accompanied by great festivity and ritual that screened the normal lifestyle of his people from his view. Within the walls of his summer palace, the Norbulingkha, he had a private garden filled with plants and wild animals that roamed free. His winter palace, the Potala, was considerably more bleak inside, even though it was one of the most beautiful buildings in the world from the outside. An insatiably curious teenager, he often sat on his roof with a telescope trying to observe everyday life in the town below, longing to be a part of the lightness and laughter.

Some ice skates left behind by a departing British legation helped bring the Dalai Lama and Harrer together. (In this book you'll find several variations on the exact events leading up to their first meeting. They haven't been "cleaned up" into complete consistency, because they're all true. In their variety they reflect real-life history filtered by forty-plus years of memory.) Being a great lover of fun and sport, Harrer founded a skating club with some Tibetan friends on a frozen pond not far from the Potala. The sight of robed monks flailing and crashing on the ice astonished and amused the populace. Monks, children, and even one of the Dalai Lama's older brothers, Lobsang Samten, joined in the fun. When the crowd laughed uproariously, the sound drifted upward in the quiet winter air to the quarters of the Dalai Lama, who couldn't quite see the frozen pond from his rooftop observation post.

The thirteen-year-old Dalai Lama heard about the new sport from his brother and tried to figure out a way to see this "walking on knives" for himself. Because protocol made it impossible for him to go there personally, he came up with a novel plan. Out of the blue he sent a small 16mm movie camera to Harrer, whom he had never met, with instructions to film the skating. The first film took two months to process in India. The Dalai Lama responded to it with tremendous interest and a critical eye, which was evident in his messages to do more films of different subjects and in his precise directions about how to make the best use of light and form. Thus Harrer became the

Dalai Lama's personal photographer before the two actually met.

Harrer tried to avoid being conspicuous with the movie camera, especially at festivals and religious ceremonies. He operated on his own feelings and the Dalai Lama's expressed desire for candid films. As it became known that Harrer was working at the request of His Holiness, the filming became less candid. Like a modern press photographer, he was given special access to events and an open field of view. He discovered the power of the camera to alter its own reality through such incidents as asking the most stern and feared Tibetan guards to pose for him. Their gruff demeanor instantly faded away and "they obeyed like lambs." And wherever Harrer took the Dalai Lama's movie camera, the little Leica was with him too.

The one exception was when he went to see the Dalai Lama; then he always left the cameras behind. "I thought it was better to keep this friendship and my ability to see him," Harrer says today. He saw many scenes that he knew would have made lovely photographs, such as "when the giant door leading into the Yellow Wall was secretly opened and through the opening crack there peeked a monk, and above him, His Holiness was gazing down on me." He also reflects, "I was always rather disappointed that foreigners who came for a few days were permitted to take pictures of His Holiness, while I never got to do it." Harrer's trade-off was well worth it in the end.

As the two Austrians stayed on in Lhasa, their status improved. They became permanent residents and officials of the Tibetan government. Aufschnaiter worked as an engineer on the construction of a small hydroelectric plant, a dam, and some canals. They planted willows to provide wood fuel for the frequent festivals without damaging native trees. But when Harrer began to work personally with the Dalai Lama, he felt that his "life in Lhasa had entered a new phase. My existence had an aim. I no longer felt unsatisfied or incomplete."

"Many people say I was a tutor of His Holiness," Harrer comments, "but I don't. We were just friends and he was interested to hear from me. I had a chance, for the first time in my life, to use my training as a geography teacher. The Dalai Lama was brought up by monks who had never left Tibet. They taught him religion, meditation, and whatever was important then to the Tibetan government. And suddenly along comes Harrer and explains how the earth is round. How to shake hands. Science and geography. . . . I was the link between his medieval world and his future life in the West."

During the five years that Harrer and Aufschnaiter were in Lhasa, the power structure within Asia changed more drastically than it had in the previous 500 years.

In August 1947, the British formally gave up their control of India and prepared to leave the subcontinent after the strength of Mahatma Gandhi's nonviolent philosophy of *ahimsa* proved too much for their weary empire to endure. The Dalai Lama very much believed in Gandhi's ways, but he also took notice of the violence that followed in the wake of Gandhi's assassination and British attempts to establish two new independent nations out of old India. What separated predominately Hindu India from Muslim Pakistan was less a border than a festering wound along an arbitrary line drawn by the British when they gave the two countries their "freedom at midnight." Millions died in the fighting that ensued. When the fighting spread to the Himalayan mountain kingdom of Kashmir, where the British hadn't extended their arbitrary line, the two countries drew their own by sword. The United Nations was called in to monitor a "cease-fire line" along this boundary. To avoid putting United Nations observers virtually on ice, the line stopped about a hundred miles southwest of Tibet in the middle of glacier-draped peaks where no humans had ever lived. This set a precedent not only for the Dalai Lama's appeals to the United Nations just two years later, but also for that body's failure to take a stand in Tibet.

In early 1950, the Dalai Lama's eldest brother, Tagtser Rinpoche, traveled overland 1,000 miles with a dire warning. The Chinese were coming. The People's Liberation Army had already seized Kumbum Monastery near the Dalai Lama's birthplace in northeast Tibet, where Tagtser Rinpoche was the head lama. The Chinese authorities had asked Tagtser Rinpoche to tell his brother to give up the throne, demanding that he kill the Dalai Lama if this did not happen. If he cooperated, they said, he would be installed in his brother's place as the governor of Tibet.

Instead, the courageous Tagtser Rinpoche warned his brother to arm the populace and prepare for war. The young Dalai Lama would not consider a militant strategy. It violated the Buddhist tradition of compassion toward all sentient beings, a tradition that had been nurtured toward philosophical perfection in the rare air and empty spaces of Tibet. The Dalai Lama, who believed in the power of positive thought, had had no experience to make him think there were people he and his countrymen could not get along with. Tagtser Rinpoche firmly told him that he would not be able to reason with the Chinese Communists and that they would lose their country unless they fought or got outside help.

After the Dalai Lama's unsuccessful appeal to the United Nations in 1950, he tried to open up discourse with the Chinese. Meanwhile, Tagtser Rinpoche gave up his lama's robes, left Tibet on a quest to save his homeland, and took back his informal name of Norbu. But that is another story—wonderfully told in *Tibet Is My Country*, written jointly by Harrer and Thubten Jigme Norbu, the former Tagtser Rinpoche, who went on to become a professor at Indiana University.

Harrer's narratives are full of the same decisive life force that permeates his being, even in old age. From behind the facade of an eighty-year-old man in a sports jacket, dancing blue eyes peer with the eager anticipation of a child. Before meeting Harrer, I had not planned to bring myself into these introductory comments. After meeting him, I changed my mind.

Just before flying to New York City in October 1991 to meet Harrer for the first time—at the opening of an exhibition of some of the photographs in this book—I took my customary Tuesday run with a neighbor. As we ran, I mentioned that I was finally getting to meet one of my heroes, someone he had probably never heard of—a mountain climber who crossed Tibet and had taught the Dalai Lama.

"What's his name?" my friend Brian asked.

"Heinrich Harrer."

"I know exactly who he is. When I was a teenager, I used to carry a quote from his book *The White Spider* about willing yourself to push the limits of the possible. I read it for inspiration before every race." Brian Maxwell went on to become Canada's best marathoner and a member of the Olympic team.

I remember a similar "chance" happening in 1975 in a hotel room in Pakistan. While held down by bad weather before flying across the Himalaya to begin an expedition to K2, I happened to meet the American zoologist George Schaller, the major character in Peter Matthiessen's bestseller *The Snow Leopard*. We spent the entire night talking about the Himalaya, its wildlife, and Tibet, where Schaller wanted to go more than any place in the world.

In 1954, Schaller had attended a lecture on Tibet while a student at the University of Alaska. When he learned that guest lecturer Heinrich Harrer was looking for a climbing companion, he volunteered to join him on the first ascent of Mount Drum, a glacier-laden volcano that rises 12,000 feet from almost sea level in the Wrangell Range. While on the climb, Harrer told Schaller about the wildlife he'd seen in Tibet and how plentiful and virtually unafraid the animals were.

Schaller's interest had been fired. During our conversation twenty-one years later, he told me about his passion to someday explore Tibet and survey its wild animals. On U.S.

Army maps drawn from satellite imagery he had seen recently built roads tracing much of Harrer's route across Tibet. When Tibet opened to the West five years after our meeting, Schaller began his quest; he has now spent most of the last twelve years surveying Tibet's remaining wildlife, which the Chinese occupation has decimated into a shadow of its former glory. In the wild, roadless plains of the Changthang in the northeast, he found large herds much as Harrer had seen them, and in 1990 convinced the Chinese to set aside a huge nature reserve the size of Colorado.

These indirect but very personal contacts with Harrer's legacy were only part of what made me feel as if I had known him all my life before we finally met in New York. As we talked, my thoughts went back to the summer of 1955 when I turned fifteen. My father had given me a copy of *Seven Years in Tibet* to take on a two-week wilderness trip. I remembered reading it and doing a little climbing, but I had no memory of consciously trying to follow Harrer's footsteps. Yet the parallels since then are remarkable. I have climbed big routes in my home mountains, gone to the Himalaya, traveled through Tibet, met the Dalai Lama, written books about Tibet, and photographed the country; I still climb there for the fun of it. The places we have both gone, the people we have met, and the things we have done coincide at so many points that it would be easy for me to speculate on a mystical connection. But neither Harrer nor I incline toward mysticism, and neither of us is a practicing Buddhist. We both take pride in our practical, no-nonsense natures. Fate or destiny did not bring Harrer from India to Lhasa; he had consciously willed it to happen. Similarly, my meeting with Harrer happened because of lifetimes of choices we both made. On the most basic level, those choices have kept us alive, despite our adventurous lifestyles.

In the introduction he wrote for *Seven Years in Tibet,* the great British explorer Peter Fleming declares, "It is the luckiest of chances that Herr Harrer should have had, and should have made such admirable use of, the opportunity to study on intimate terms a people with whom the West is now denied . . . contacts." Harrer, of course, disagrees about the role of luck and chance, insisting that every "lucky" event in his life has been foregrounded by thorough preparation, including his ability to survive the two years spent crossing Tibet. Still, one cannot help wondering about the role of chance in Harrer's finding a hundred meters of unexposed film. Without that film, would we be holding this extraordinary, enduring book of pictures of a Lhasa that is lost forever? And would we have had one more chance to hear from the man whose visionary eye and hand captured these precious moments?

# THE STORY

*In the Dolomites, 1934*

# MOUNTAIN DREAMS

Once, when I was visiting the young Fourteenth Dalai Lama in Lhasa, he said to me, "You know, when somebody brings an application up to my seat in the uppermost story of the Potala, he has to go up step by step. He has to climb up and up for many hundreds of steps until he can finally hand it over to me." I think that life is the same. You can't jump directly from the ground floor up to the tenth floor in the Potala, and you can't do it in life either: You have to go up gradually, step by step.

I was born in 1912 near the villages of Knappenberg and Hüttenberg, in what was then the Carinthia region of the Austro-Hungarian Empire—and is now southern Austria. I never knew a life of prosperity—quite the opposite, in fact. And I never had time to play, because I always had to do something. I had to pluck berries, of which we had enormous numbers in the garden; or fetch wood or water; or help in the kitchen. It was understood that I would do these chores in addition to going to school. Our village was tiny. Most of the few hundred men who lived there worked in an underground iron mine. But my grandfather had a little farm and my mother's mother came from peasant stock.

I felt sheltered in the harmony of a great family, and I have wonderful memories from my early years. From our village we could see limestone mountains far to the south. I wanted to go there one day, for I already had the idea that I would like to see really big mountains and exotic countries with foreign people. My uncle collected little books telling of people with different customs and skin colors. I have long felt that the important dreams of life begin in youth—and here, looking at my uncle's books and at the distant mountains, is where my own dreams began.

Later I went to secondary school in nearby Graz, followed by studies at the university there. This was when I started skiing, making my own skis from the wooden planks of wine barrels. At first I engaged in many sports and did well in track and field. Training came naturally, because I often had to run ten miles just to get to the local competitions; in the evening I ran home again. I won a few prizes—not trophies or money, but usually wreaths that I would give to my parents, who seemed very happy about it. One day I came home with my wreath, but it was made from oak leaves and not laurel, as was usual. My mother didn't even glance at it; she just put it aside. Much later she told me she had been disappointed because she couldn't use the oak leaves to spice her dishes, which is what she did with the laurel.

I'm convinced I got a lot of what Thomas Mann called "prenatal merits" from my mother's ancestors. I had the ambition to be better than the others and to have the will to follow a goal. Later I called this, "have a plan and stick to it," which has been one of my guiding philosophies. As a young man I eventually discovered that to become the best in a sport, I had to concentrate. I decided I would ski during the winter and climb in summer.

Five years went by and some of my long-range plans began materializing. A good downhill racer, I was invited to join the Austrian Olympic Team for the 1936 Winter Games in Garmisch-Partenkirchen. The next year I won the downhill event at the World Student Championships. In the summer I did many difficult climbs, but I also had to pay for it: one day I barely survived a 170-foot fall. Some of my climbing companions had already fallen to their deaths in the mountains. Gradually my climbs became more and more difficult as every year I visited the Dolomites or the Western Alps, and I often made first ascents.

*I was raised on the mountainside near the village of Knappenberg. Here my parents and I are with my baby brother Josef and my sister Lydia.*

My father was just a simple postal officer, but my mother managed to save money for my university studies. Along with sports, I studied geography, a field that certainly helped me later in life. During my student days I also became a member of the Austrian Alpine Club, where I learned about the Himalaya; I loved the understated style of the British expedition books. By studying geography, I became acquainted with explorers like Alexander von Humboldt, who became a role model. I also loved to read books by the legendary Swedish explorer Sven Hedin, who once came to give a lecture at the University of Graz. After the lecture I collected his autograph, the only one I have ever asked for in my life. I shall never forget the moment when he looked at me and asked what I was studying. And one day I read the works of Alfred Wegener, who had developed the then-controversial theory of continental drift. I think it is wonderful to have role models like these people I admired.

My expeditions in Europe grew bigger and bigger, and I made ever more new and difficult ascents. In 1937 I got to know Fritz Kasparek from Vienna. We made some difficult climbs together, then decided we should try the unclimbed north face of Eiger. I was highly ambitious; I often thought that if you can be the first, it doesn't particularly matter what you are the first at. In mountaineering you have a lot of chances to be the first—at least you did during the 1930s when I grew up.

The story of our first ascent on the Eiger is well known. Most of the difficult walls in the Alps had been done and the north face of Eiger was the biggest and hardest one left. It was 6,000 feet high and considered almost impossible to climb. Kasparek and I thought we could do it because we felt confident in ourselves; we were certain we would succeed. When we arrived at the wall, there were already two other chaps there attempting what so many others had unsuccessfully tried to do before, some dying in the effort. We introduced ourselves to Anderl Heckmair and Ludwig Vörg and were very pleased to join forces with these superb mountaineers. The climb was certainly a credit to Heckmair, who was a tough and excellent climber; I'm sure that he even saved our lives. Before the climb we were rivals, during the climb we became partners—and now, more than fifty years later, we are still friends.

*Myself making tea [above] on the second bivouac during the first ascent of the north face of the Eiger [below]. This climb opened many opportunities for me, the most important of which was getting invited onto a Himalayan expedition.*

When we came down from our successful four-day climb, we were met by many journalists. Soon our names became known, and the next year, when I was participating in making a skiing movie in the Alps, a telegram arrived saying that I could be a member of the German and Austrian 1939 Himalayan expedition, a reconnaissance to Nanga Parbat in what is now Pakistan but was then part of India. This was my big dream; in fact, I climbed the Eiger hoping that this would get me invited on a Himalayan expedition—after all, I had no money to pay my own way. I had even turned down important job offers that would have kept me from going to the Himalaya if I was invited. So when the

news came that I could go—provided I could leave in four days—I was very excited. I quit the film immediately and joined the expedition in Antwerp. The leader of our group was Peter Aufschnaiter, a well-known Austrian mountaineer who had participated in the Kangchenjunga, Nepal expeditions of 1929 and 1931.

After many months of reconnaissance around and on Nanga Parbat, we eventually arrived in Karachi, India (in present-day Pakistan). This was on August 8, 1939. The freighter that was to take us home didn't arrive. War seemed imminent, and we were in

British territory. A proclamation had just come out that no foreigner could leave the main trunk roads or main railways. Anyone who did would be subject to a ten-year prison sentence. But I tried to escape toward Persia with two companions. We slipped away from our guards and drove north a few hundred miles through the desert. But the British captured us and brought us back to the superintendent of police in Karachi.

We had violated the rule on travel, of course, but the superintendent said to us, "Well, gentlemen, you lost your way while hunting, didn't you?"

We looked at each other and finally one of us said, "Yes, sir!" So that was it, and we went to have a beer in the garden together. But a few days later, when hostilities began, we were arrested and put behind barbed wire.

Later we were transferred to another camp, this one near Bombay. Then we were shipped farther north in India, to a place called Deolali. Much later we were moved to yet another camp, this one near Dehra Dun, in the foothills of the Himalaya. I was back near the mountains at last.

*Himalayan wildflower*

*The Western Gate to Lhasa, through*
*which we entered the Holy City in rags after*
*our two-year journey across Tibet.*

# ESCAPE TO TIBET

Even before reaching Dehra Dun, I had already tried escaping, without success. But here in the foothills of the Himalaya, I knew without a doubt that I would try to flee north across the mountains to Tibet—even though I had read that the people there were rather inhospitable to foreign travelers.

Fortunately, our little group of conspirators had a Tibetan dictionary and some books and maps. The officials in Karachi who had searched our luggage hadn't cared about such material. The maps were crude, but they were maps. I started studying Japanese in case I should get through to allies of the Austrian forces. I also studied Hindi to get along while in India and, naturally, learned a few words of Tibetan.

I tried to escape several times in 1943. The British attitude about escape attempts was that they were all right if you did them in a sporting style; in that case they treated you tolerantly. But if you tried to cheat them—as when they were unarmed on an excursion—then you were punished much more severely.

One time, after I had been caught following a month of freedom, our camp's commandant, Colonel Williams, lectured me. "You made a daring escape, Mr. Harrer. I admire you, but I still have to give you twenty-eight days solitary confinement in accordance with the Geneva Convention." He sent me to a cell with a wooden plank to sleep on. Every day I had to go out for a seven-hour work detail. An unarmed sergeant major came with me. He sat in the shade while I dug ditches, then filled them in again. "Mr. Harrer," he would say, "don't work so hard. It doesn't matter what you do, you just have to do *something*." I told him I had to train for my next escape, which only made him laugh. He would then take myself to the kitchen, where we'd be served the finest cuts of meat—much better than what the other prisoners ate. After twenty-eight days of such treatment, I was fit and well fed.

(Many years later, shortly after my book *Seven Years in Tibet* came out, I gave a lecture in the Royal Festival Hall in London. I read a letter to the audience that I found lying on the podium. It was from the same Colonel Williams, and it said, "As commander of your camp, I had to take the blame for your successful escape. Tonight, to add insult to injury, I had to pay to listen to you tell how you did it." The audience roared with laughter.)

On April 29, 1944, Peter Aufschnaiter and I, along with five others, made our final breakout. Two prisoners split off immediately for the lowlands; five of us made it to Tibet after a harrowing eighteen-day journey. We crossed into the notorious "Forbidden Country" at a 17,200-foot-high pass. Here a stone cairn and prayer flags indicated that we stood facing an entirely different world.

The air was thin and our stomachs empty; we saw nothing but mountains and ice and snow. The only fuels we could find to build fires to fight off the frigid nights were some thorny bushes and a little dried cow dung. But we enjoyed a new sense of security because we knew the British were powerless here: Tibet was a neutral country.

The first people we met were just as inhospitable as we had heard. The Tibetans had a simple way of keeping out foreigners: they didn't give you fuel for building fires, and they didn't give you food. Without these two things, proceeding was difficult. They never had police, customs guards, or military along their border.

*Cold winds raced down from the mountains and across Tibet's plains, enabling flapping prayer flags to send their messages heavenward.*

After several days of walking we reached a village called Tsaparang, famous in Tibet's history because in the seventeenth century some Catholic missionaries had established a small church there. We could find no trace of the church. In the same town an unfriendly local official told us he'd give us food, transport, and fuel only if we went back to India; otherwise we would get nothing. Using the universal finger-across-the-throat sign, he indicated that the government would slice off his head if he let us continue inside his country.

While debating what to do, we explored our surroundings. Cliffs rose everywhere around Tsaparang, and caves at their bases were filled with offerings. Thousands of devotional clay figurines called *tsatsa* lay around, along with fragments of old manuscripts and books. One day we opened an ancient door and looked down upon a tall, golden Buddha.

After days of negotiations, the official finally agreed that we could go to the town of Shangtse and thence into India. He gave us a soldier and some donkeys. And so we marched through this far-western part of Tibet, a fascinating region. Days later we crossed back into India, as required by the officials, at a low pass near Shipki.

We had been gone from India about six weeks, and we felt that even if we had to go back to our prison camp, our hardships had been worthwhile. The soldier and the donkey driver who accompanied us gave us encouraging words at the frontier, telling us of Lhasa with its pretty girls and good beer. "Perhaps one day we shall meet in Lhasa," the donkey man said with a smile.

We were determined not to go back behind barbed wire, so when we reached Namgya, the first village in British territory, we said we were American soldiers on leave. We bought new provisions (we had earned money in the internment camp in various ways) and again headed north, past towering, ice-covered mountains. Soon we realized that we had crossed into Tibet again. Here we pretended we were British soldiers on leave and told them we intended to go to the holy mountain of Kailas.

We soon saw enormous herds of yaks, and in one of the herders' tents we were hospitably received. A young nomad with a pigtail said that if we wouldn't tell anybody, he knew where to get wonderful game. With an old muzzleloading musket, some lead bullets, and some gunpowder, he took us hunting in the nearby mountains. He shot at lots of wild sheep but missed every time. Instead of sheep, we collected handfuls of wild onions. Back in the tent, the nomad's wife laughed; she was used to her husband's misfortunes. She picked up an enormous piece of aging venison and started preparing us a wonderful meal. When her heavy fur garment hindered her movements, she surprised us by stripping down to her waist and carrying on happily.

We enjoyed the freedom of this life, for we had been prisoners for so long, and so we stayed on one more day with these hospitable people—the first friendly Tibetans we had met. We were not afraid of being caught here since we were far from any British influence or Tibetan officials.

All too soon we descended to the upper Indus Valley. Along the way we saw large herds of *kyangs*, beautiful wild asses. Two stallions fought as their mares danced about. It was an unforgettable sight, one we would often see later on.

Our group of ex-prisoners was now down to three, Aufschnaiter, Hans Kopp, and me; the others had split off during the previous weeks. We marched together alongside the tiny Indus River for five days before arriving at Gartok, the capital of a province in western Tibet, a place said to be the highest capital in the world, well over 13,000 feet. As we neared this site, we saw a few tents and mud huts—that was all. This was a capital city?

We entered one of these ramshackle dwellings and met the local governor. He was a true nobleman, quite unlike the provincial official we'd met in the first village after leaving India. The atmosphere was pleasant, and he gave us tea and dried fruits. Our conversation was fluent because by this time we had learned quite a number of Tibetan words. We mentioned that we were not pilgrims, but prisoners of war and that Tibet was a neutral country where we would like to stay.

After I gave this man a few presents, he said he had a colleague. We knew, of course, about Tibetan government officials; there were always a minimum of two with the same rank, one a lay person and one a monk, and this man said his colleague was on a pilgrimage to Mt. Kailas. He would soon return, and then the pair would decide whether or not we could travel through their province.

Soon the other fellow arrived, and he went first to a monastery chapel to thank his God for his safe arrival. After a couple more days of waiting and negotiating, the two governors gave us permission to travel within their province if we would then cross into neutral Nepal. We had to swear that we would not continue our travel out of their region toward central Tibet. They also gave us permission to buy food. Even more important, we could also buy yak dung to make fires at the caravan stations en route.

At last, on July 13, we bade farewell to Gartok, accompanied by some Tibetans and possessing an extremely valuable travel document. After days of easy and comfortable walking along the caravan route that connects western and central Tibet, we fell into a routine. We would pitch our little tent in the early evening and have warm tea. The next morning we would march on to one of several caravan sites, where we would change animals.

Finally, we reached the holiest of all the holy mountains in the world, Mt. Kailas. Although only about 22,000 feet high, this is surely one of the most beautiful mountains in the world. At a sacred lake called Manasarovar I tried to take a bath, but I fell into a swamp and started sinking. I threw myself flat on the mud and rocked myself back into safety.

Later, we crossed a pass and arrived at the upper reaches of Tibet's largest river: the Brahmaputra, or, in Tibetan, the Tsangpo. It was fascinating to travel in the region so well described by my old hero, Sven Hedin.

Soon we reached a place called Tradün. Here, in this caravan town, we were received warmly because of our special travel papers and our ability to communicate: our Tibetan skills had greatly improved, especially Peter Aufschnaiter's, who already spoke it fluently.

In Tradün we met two high officials from Lhasa who were collecting taxes from the big caravan route. They were beautifully dressed in yellow silk-and-brocade robes. We ate with them and they promised to send a letter to Lhasa for us, asking for permission to travel farther east. They suggested that instead of going into Nepal, we should stay in a room in Tradün until word from Lhasa arrived.

We made many excursions in the ensuing weeks; sometimes we sketched the two famous mountains we could see rising in the south, Dhaulagiri and Annapurna. We saw many different animals, including gazelles, herds of which roamed across the high plateau.

By this time we realized that the higher the rank of the officials we met, the easier they were to negotiate with. They were all considerate and seemed to understand our position. But weeks turned into months as we waited for the reply from the capital. We began to lose patience and get on each other's nerves. Hans Kopp opted to head for Nepal, leaving in late November.

Now only Peter Aufschnaiter and I were left from the original group. Lamas who came through with the caravans told us that it was only two-and-a-half months from Tradün to Lhasa, so Aufschnaiter and I kept dreaming of continuing our trip toward the "Forbidden City."

Finally, in December 1944, after four months in Tradün, news came from Lhasa that we had official permission to go via the shortest route to Nepal. What we had feared had come true: they didn't want us to proceed through Inner Tibet. So we said farewell to our many new friends in Tradün. They gave us food, and we had some horses and yaks to carry our belongings. They also gave us many yak loads of dried dung, and we needed it: the temperature was ten degrees Fahrenheit. A soldier accompanied us, carrying our official travel document wrapped like a sacred relic; he was to deliver this to the governor of Kyirong, near the Nepalese frontier. We were curious to see this document and so one day

*Throughout our journey we would come across large flocks of sheep. Their wool was Tibet's most important export.*

when the soldier was sleeping, we carefully opened the letter. Aufschnaiter made a copy of it and we sealed it up again. Later, he translated it. It said we were on our way to Nepal and that people should help us with provisions.

We crossed some high, cold passes and after a week reached Dzongka on Christmas Day. With a hundred mud-brick huts clustered around a monastery, this was the first real town we had encountered. We got a room and soon a leg of mutton was boiling in our cooking pot. We celebrated the holiday by lighting a few butter lamps.

According to our travel documents, we were supposed to leave the next morning, but we were fortunate: by dawn two feet of fresh snow had fallen. There would be no possibility of leaving with our yak caravan to travel farther south. We spent a month in Dzongka, making excursions around the town.

When the weather finally cleared, it was frigid, but we were asked to leave because a large yak caravan was heading in the direction we were supposed to go. Ahead of us in the deep snow, yaks acted as snowplows, clearing the way. As we descended through valleys and villages, it got somewhat warmer: we were approaching the tropical zone.

Eventually we arrived in Kyirong, the "village of happiness." I shall never cease thinking about the beauties of this place, which lay just north of the Nepalese frontier. The surroundings were incredible. Kyirong was about 10,000 feet high and around it were woods with rhododendrons and other flowering trees. The eighty-odd houses looked something like those in Switzerland because they had slanted roofs and the shingles were weighted down by stones to keep them from blowing off. Instead of chimneys, however, the roofs were marked with prayer flags.

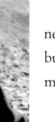

*The extended tongue shows respect and is a traditional greeting to one of higher rank.*

We were quartered in a very small room, so small that I preferred the nearby barn. Aufschnaiter took the room, coping with rats and bugs; but I had to contend with mice and fleas. All this, of course, really didn't matter, for we were still free in Tibet.

The local governor had read our travel documents and expected us to leave soon for Nepal, but Aufschnaiter and I didn't like the idea of ending up behind barbed wire again, as would probably happen if we continued to Nepal, so we applied for another stay. He agreed, saying he would write an application and send it to Lhasa. Of course, we knew this would take a long time, so we waited happily with this reprieve.

We made excursions in all directions, visiting monasteries and the meadows up in the mountains. Everywhere we were received with great kindness. We got butter to eat, we visited hermits and monasteries, and we explored all the valleys around Kyirong. In some we found enormous numbers of wild strawberries, but unfortunately we also discovered beastly leeches. These are the plague of many Himalayan valleys, and we were helpless against them. They would even creep through the eyelets of our shoes.

Months passed in Kyirong. Springtime came and went. The local governor finally received a message from Lhasa: we were supposed to leave soon for Nepal. In the meantime, we had heard that the war was over, but we still knew we would be imprisoned if we went back to India. We promised the governor to leave in the autumn, though we didn't tell him of our secret plan, which was to continue our journey toward Lhasa.

Soon it was November and our permitted term of residence was coming to an end; we had been in Kyirong for more than ten months. Our departure was dramatic. The people realized that we were not planning to go south toward Nepal, and, scared of the local officials, they tried to prevent us from leaving. But by this time we were determined to go. So Aufschnaiter went first, and a few days later, under the cover of night, I managed to leave town and rendezvous with Peter. That night, for the last time in many years, we slept in a forest.

We crossed back over the mountains once again, this time bypassing Dzongka. Winter arrived as we carefully wound northward, skirting villages and often traveling at night to avoid detection. We crossed the Tsangpo at Chung Rivoche, and everyone we met warned us not to go further north; the brigands living up there would certainly kill us. But we disregarded these warnings and moved north for weeks, in temperatures as low as forty below zero. Our motto by this time was, "On to Lhasa!"

To avoid large cites, we decided to move even farther north, into the Changthang region—the famous Tibetan Plateau. Here we would see only nomads and brigands; government officials avoided the area. We were setting out into terra incognita, and a feeling in the pit of my stomach reminded me of how I felt the night before tackling the north face of the Eiger.

For days we traveled northeast into the unknown, facing snowstorms, hunger, frostbite. Aufschnaiter and I had long talks about turning back. Our yak was starving and we could not go on without him. We resolved to keep on for one more day, and then to make a decision. Fortunately, we crossed a pass and descended into a snowless region with ample grazing for our poor yak.

We encountered nomads often; we ate in their tents, got warm in front of their fires, and learned about their primitive way of life. Their entire lives are organized so as to make the most of the scanty aids to living that nature provides on the Changthang.

It was still bitterly cold as we marched onward toward the "Forbidden City," making as much as twenty miles on a good day. The nights were absolutely miserable; we lay close together, unable to sleep because of the cold and the countless lice that crawled over our emaciated bodies.

One day we encountered brigands; we had been warned about these cruel rebels who would even kill you for your possessions, but we hadn't taken the advice seriously. The robbers tried to separate us but we noticed the ruse and managed to get away—barely. We would have given anything for a rifle, but we had almost run out of money. We carefully avoided their encampments from then on.

One day we crested a ridge; ahead was the loneliest landscape we had ever seen. A sea of snowy mountains stretched onward endlessly. We loped for hours across virgin snow in temperatures that might have been as low as forty below zero. I was tormented by visions of warm, comfortable rooms and delicious hot food.

The next day, fortunately, we met a caravan of friendly nomads and traveled with them toward Lhasa, now fairly close. They moved too slowly for our taste, however, and after a few days we set out on our own again. It was Christmas Eve, 1945.

During the next few weeks we met more nomads and brigands. We were not generally harassed by the latter since we looked so wretched, especially after our yak was stolen one night and we were reduced to walking along like starving beggars.

The final obstacle before Lhasa was a formidable 20,000-foot pass called Guring La. A pilgrimage path across it was used all year round, and we saw many pilgrims. The fact that we had no travel papers made no difference; apparently it was assumed that foreigners who got this far into Tibet must obviously possess a permit. The closer we got to the capital, the less trouble we had. We met up with various nomads and military outfits and traveled with them in relative luxury.

Then, one fine day in mid-January, we came out onto the plains of Lhasa. The Holy City lay just ahead.

*Wearing a cap some would claim is made of
yeti skin, this itinerant man carries many
charms on his spear. Though not a monk,
he lives for his religion, traveling from festival
to festival all year long.*

*Washing the gold-plated lions on top of the
Potala. Immediately below is the village of Shö.*

# LHASA

When we first spied the golden roofs of the Potala, the winter residence of the Dalai Lama, we felt like kneeling down and thanking the gods. We had been twenty-one months on the way and had crossed sixty-five mountain passes. We thought of our adventures and of our comrades still in the internment camp at Dehra Dun.

Immediately after our arrival—on January 15, 1946—we were placed under a kind of house arrest in the home of a man named Thangme, a nobleman who befriended us the moment we reached the Holy City. Within a day, however, we were given clothes, all the food we could eat, and even haircuts! At the same time, Thangme talked with the higher authorities, who said we wouldn't be deported. But they politely requested that we stay indoors until the Regent, the man who was ruling the country until the Dalai Lama came of age, decided our future. We were delighted; a few days' rest was exactly what we needed.

Eight days passed. Then, to our surprise, we were invited to meet the parents of His Holiness, the Dalai Lama. This meeting went extremely well, and loaded with gifts and escorted by servants, we returned to Thangme's house. Our stock rose considerably after visiting the holy parents, and soon we were free to go into the city.

We made a point of paying courtesy visits to the four cabinet ministers, on whose good favor our continued stay in Lhasa depended. We noticed during these meetings that the dignitaries often smiled with amusement when we spoke with them; later we discovered that they found our strange dialect very funny—we spoke like the farmers and nomads we had associated with for a year and a half.

After staying nearly a month in Thangme's house, we were invited by Tsarong, a celebrated minister, to move into a bungalow in his compound. This gave us more room, and we greatly appreciated the gesture.

Peter Aufschnaiter, with his polite demeanor and modesty, was well liked in Lhasa, especially by the monks. It was a hopeful omen for our future when a few months after our arrival he was summoned by a high monastic official and commissioned to build an irrigation canal. Aufschnaiter was an agricultural engineer, so he really was able to help; he soon taught workers the principles of building irrigation ditches.

During that first year I also made myself useful, designing and creating new gardens. I built a fountain for Tsarong's family; I gave lessons in various subjects; and sometimes I went out of town to help Aufschnaiter with his canal work. During these times the local people were so curious that they surrounded us to watch what we were doing.

*Peter Aufschnaiter [top] measured distances from the Chagpori during our mapping of Lhasa. We had planned to install a sewage system for the city. Tibetans invited me to all their parties, so I entertained them in turn with Christmas in my home [below].*

We were once asked to devise ways of improving the sewage system and water pipelines. Aufschnaiter told them that before we began, we'd have to have an accurate map of the Holy City. This proved to be unforgettable work. Using an old theodolite we had found, Aufschnaiter created a map of Lhasa and its surroundings as far down as Norbulingkha, the summer palace. I visited all the houses in the city and measured their interiors, calculated the sizes of the shops, and so on.

There was little wood in the region; the forests had long since been destroyed. Dried animal dung was used to make small fires to heat water and food, but firewood for heating purposes was unknown. We could warm our cold hands only by dipping them into an earthenware pot filled with warm ashes from the kitchen. Meanwhile, I suffered greatly from sciatica, perhaps because I had slept on one side on the frozen ground in central Tibet. A local doctor told me to sit on the edge of a chair and roll a stick back and forth with my bare feet. This helped, and when the weather got warmer I was cured.

Early on we lived always with the fear that the authorities would ask us to leave. Indeed, they sometimes came to talk with us, saying that the British legation was requesting that we leave the country. But we had long ago learned the customs of Tibet: given enough time, things would work out. We wrote a new application, which took months to negotiate. After a year and a half they stopped asking us questions—and only then could we relax and live happily like the Tibetans themselves.

By then Aufschnaiter had been asked if he could improve the local electric plant, which worked only occasionally, and he lived there, outside of town. But when Christmas 1946 came around, he stayed with me in Lhasa. We decided to give a Christmas party, and a friend of mine said we could use his house. I decorated a tiny juniper with candles, apples, nuts, and sweets; it looked very much like the real thing.

I invited a number of friends and we passed the evening eating, drinking, and playing games. After we played "Silent Night" on the record player, I must confess that I had a sudden attack of homesickness.

We soon adjusted our way of living; in Tibet there was no rush and no stress. We had plenty of time to become friendly with the famous families of Lhasa. I lived in Tsarong's house, where I had a beautiful room with a big window, but I soon exchanged my Tibetan furniture for European designs; no longer did I have to sit cross-legged on low cushions. I set up a writing table, on which I kept my detailed diary. Unfortunately, as I became accustomed to life in Lhasa, I lost interest in writing, thinking that I would remember everything—which is, of course, not the case.

I attended many big parties, which lasted for days, sometimes weeks. I began to give parties in return; mine often lasted three days because the first day you could invite only the highest officers. The next two days were reserved for the lesser ranks. We would borrow little tables and cushions from other houses—and also their cooks. I spent most of my money on these parties because I thought I should give something in return for the hospitality the people had shown us.

I would say that there is no other country in the world where two fugitives would be as welcomed as we were in Lhasa. The British Mission, located just outside town, also became friendly with us after a while. Eventually they permitted us to send our mail via the British representative to India. This means of communication was rather complicated, but it did get letters to Europe. So, three years after our escape, our families heard for the first time that we were alive and that we lived happily in Tibet.

*My house in Tsarong's compound. The mountain in the background is Gephe Utse, which rises behind the Drepung Monastery.*

As the years went by, we became a part of Lhasa and were employed by the government, receiving a monthly salary from the foreign office. We took part in local events whenever we could. One of my favorites was what one could call a "festival of light," or Ganden Ngamchö. This event, which took place in the middle of December, honored Tsong Khapa, the Reformer, the Founder of the Yellow Sect (the Gelug Order) whose tomb was in Ganden Monastery. Thousands upon thousands of butter lights covered the flat roofs of Lhasa. Not only was Lhasa full of lights: the surrounding mountains and all the big monasteries were as well. It reminded me of Europe on June 21, when we would go up into the mountains and light fires on the ridges and summits. In Lhasa the main ceremony took place on the inner ring road called the Barkor. The Dalai Lama walked slowly around the street, always clockwise. Following him were the ministers and high-ranking monks and officers, among whom I recognized many of my friends. All were carrying smoking incense sticks. Nobody is supposed to be higher than the Dalai Lama, so the rooftops were empty; I hid in the first floor of one of my friends' houses and watched the proceedings. The townspeople are supposed to prostrate themselves before His Holiness, but it was so crowded there was no room; instead, they simply bowed in respect. I had seen these kinds of obeisance to the Tibetan Living God before, but I was always impressed. It was a vision from another world.

*The Yellow Wall in the Norbulingkha. Behind this wall was the holy sanctum where the Dalai Lama lived. In the foreground one can see that these gardens were a popular spot for picnicking.*

Soon I would learn much more about the life of this Living God, this King of Tibet, this Fourteenth Dalai Lama. During the time I worked to improve the Holy Mother's gardens, I became close friends with Lobsang Samten, an older brother of His Holiness. Lobsang was one of the privileged few who went up to the Potala to speak freely with his brother. He told His Holiness what we were doing together—swimming and ice skating and other fun activities; the Dalai Lama had actually seen some of this with his binoculars from high above. He, of course, was not allowed to leave his palace. One day in 1949, His Holiness sent word to his brother that he wanted me to build him a movie theater; he evidently desired to see something of the outside world and movies were his only possibility to do so.

I built the theater inside the Inner Garden of the Norbulingkha and soon thereafter came an event that seemed unbelievable: the Fourteenth Dalai Lama sent word he wanted to see me. Surprised and excited, I rode a horse down to the summer palace. First I went to the Holy Mother's bungalow; she put me at ease, telling me to go immediately to see her son. This, then, was the first time I walked through the gate of that sacred yellow wall. As it turned out, I was to visit His Holiness many more times and developed a strong friendship with the god-king.

The fifteen-year-old boy had never had playmates other than occasional visits from his siblings. Only old monks attended him, and they rarely spoke. He had teachers and tutors, but they also were old men—and none of them had ever left Tibet.

Several of these old men hovered around His Holiness as I greeted him the first time. They were as unhappy as the boy was excited: he wanted me to show some films that had just arrived. We watched movies depicting World War II, and the youth was impressed by General MacArthur; but he also admired the Japanese. I remember something else about this first meeting: His Holiness asked me, "Why do you have hair on your hands like a monkey?"

His Holiness soon asked me to make movies of events in the city, scenes he couldn't see for himself. Soon everyone in the Holy City knew that I was making films for His Holiness. I tried to keep in the background as much as possible, but the Dalai Lama always smiled at me when he was sitting on the throne or being carried in a procession.

From then on I could use horses from the stables of His Holiness, a special privilege, but rather difficult nonetheless. The horses were huge and unaccustomed to traffic; whenever I rode through the town, they would shy, often throwing me off. One wasn't allowed to ride the same horse over and over until we got used to each other.

During our unforgettable times together, certainly the best of my life, I was able to tell this young boy something about our Western culture. He was bright, curious, and full of energy. He continually astonished me by his powers of comprehension.

These years in Lhasa were a fantastic period for me, but they passed too quickly. By 1948 the Chinese Communists had already begun threatening to "liberate" Tibet. The British, meanwhile, had left Lhasa after India gained its independence. (The Indians replaced them in their mission.) These and other things—like when the giant *thangka* on the side of the Potala ripped during a windstorm—were serious omens to the Tibetans, who interpreted them as portending disaster. They erected new prayer flags and an enormous *chörten*, into which they inserted *tsatsa* offerings made of clay. Prayer wheels went up on the nearby mountains. Early in 1950, Aufschnaiter and I began stocking a secret cache high up in the mountains in order to be able to escape at a moment's notice should the Chinese make a rapid invasion.

# THE PHOTOGRAPHS

## Good-luck Scarves

Good-luck scarves, most commonly called *khatag*s, played a big part in the lives of Tibetans. When you arrived at somebody's home, said good-bye to a friend, petitioned an official, or asked for blessings from a lama, you would always have a *khatag* in your hands. The most important *khatag*s were over nine feet in length and decorated with good luck signs and wishes.

To present a *khatag*, you would hold out both of your hands, bow, and roll open the scarf. When saying good-bye, the custom was to bow, fold your hands, and almost touch foreheads with the person you gave the scarf to. Relatives would give newly married couples long, beautiful *khatag*s called *khatag ashi*. And when someone was appointed to a very high post, he would go to His Holiness the Dalai Lama to thank him for the appointment and to present him with a long *khatag*. The Dalai Lama would receive it, bless it by touching it, and return it to the newly appointed minister.

*We present khatags while saying good-bye to servants from the British Mission [left] as they leave Lhasa in a yak-hide boat (next to the dike I built with Peter Aufschnaiter). Surkhang Lhacham Kusho receives a relative in a Lhasan headdress made of coral and pearls [right].*

*Three officers greet*
*Surkhang Depön while*
*presenting him with a*
*good-luck scarf.*

A group of people ceremonially visiting an incarnate lama or even a high dignitary would lay their *khatag*s in a growing heap on his throne as they filed past. The lama wouldn't return the *khatag*s; instead he would give back colorful little strings called *sungdu*, which were like good-luck charms, worn around the neck. They had a special knot the holy man had made resembling a thunderbolt. He also blew on them as a blessing.

The most beautiful use for the *khatag* was in a religious ceremony given by high incarnate lamas, or *rinpoche*s. There came a certain moment, when he was sitting on the throne, that hundreds or thousands of *khatag*s were sent flying through the air. It was incredibly beautiful to see these *khatag*s flying toward the *rinpoche*.

*Khatag*s were also essential when you made an application to an official. You would come with a *khatag* and put forth your request. If you wanted to rise in the feudal system, say you wanted a new governorship or a new estate, then, along with the *khatag*, you put

down an envelope. In this envelope would be a note saying that if you got this or that, you would reward your benefactor later on. In this feudal system people got little or no salary, so these rewards were important.

I remember one funny time when I was given a *khatag*. When Peter Aufschnaiter and I were on our escape route to Lhasa, we received a very harsh reception from the administrator of Tsaparang Dzong, who wouldn't give us food or fuel and made us stay outside in a cave. Many months later a man came to us in Lhasa. We didn't recognize him at first, but he started prostrating in front of us, and he gave us a bag of parched barley flour and a huge piece of butter. We realized this was the man who had treated us so badly in Tsaparang. Now in Lhasa we were suddenly more powerful than he was. He also brought us very beautiful *khatag*s and tried to give us money to make us forgive him. Of course we did and we didn't want him to prostrate himself in front of us. But we felt the incident rounded out the story of our escape.

## The Dalai Lama's Family

When Peter Aufschnaiter and I reached Lhasa in 1946, we were immediately placed under a sort of house arrest in the Thangme home where we had been first taken in. One day two of the Dalai Lama's elder brothers, Norbu and Lobsang, came to tell us that their parents would like to meet us at their home. We replied that we were not allowed to leave the house. But when we told Thangme of this, he was appalled. He told us that when the Dalai Lama's family calls, you must go without hesitation.

It's not hard to imagine how our hearts were trembling as we went to visit the Holy Family at their home, called the Yapshi Tagtser. We walked down the streets looking not much different than when we first reached Lhasa, but we had the impression that everybody noticed us and everybody knew we were on our way to visit the family of His Holiness. We felt important.

We entered the large house, noticing servants everywhere, and were received very kindly by the Holy Family in the big reception room on the first floor. On the highest seat, which was really like a throne, sat Tagtser Rinpoche, otherwise known as Thubten Jigme Norbu. As an incarnate lama, he sat higher than even his own parents. Lobsang Samten interpreted for us because his parents spoke the Amdo dialect and we spoke only dialects from western Tibet (we later learned the Lhasa dialect as well).

The Holy Family gave us many wonderful gifts. First they had servants bring us loads of rice and *tsampa* and a huge ball of butter enclosed in skin. Then came two *tsugtrugs*, those famous Tibetan blankets which are made of very long wool, in which you wrap yourself for the night. Those were followed by two lambskin coats, with the wool facing inside to keep you warmer as was the Tibetan custom. They also gave us each a 100 sang note, the highest denomination in Tibet. We never spent these notes, but kept them like good-luck seeds, which kept on growing for us. This first visit proved very important; afterward we were permitted to travel freely in Lhasa.

*The incredible Holy Mother, known reverentially as Gyalyum Chemo, bore fourteen children, seven of whom survived. Three of her sons were recognized as incarnations, including the Dalai Lama himself.*

As time went by, we came to know many members of the Holy Family very well. Lobsang Samten became one of my best friends. He was a really gay man who was especially close and helpful to his brother, the Dalai Lama. When they were younger they often played together in the Potala. It was Lobsang who first took me to see the Dalai Lama and who helped me in many other ways. The Dalai Lama jokingly called us

*dzabchen,* meaning "naughty" or mischievous regarding government rules.

The Dalai Lama's father unfortunately died within a few weeks of our arrival, but his mother was always kind to us. She encouraged my visits with the Dalai Lama and even scolded me when I was late for an appointment with His Holiness. She was addressed respectfully as Gyalyum Chemo and was a very fine lady. Shortly after our arrival in

Members of the Dalai
Lama's family: His
mother is flanked by his
eldest sister, Tsering
Drölma, and his
youngest sister, Jetsün
Pemala, all in brocade
dress [far left]. His
brother Lobsang
[above] was his
principal confidant and
a fan of the games we
played in the field
outside the Holy
Family's palace [left].

Lhasa, she gave birth to the last of her fourteen children, seven of whom lived. At that time nobody yet knew that this son, too, would be discovered to be an incarnate lama (at which time he was given the name Ngari Rinpoche).

I also came to know the Dalai Lama's eldest brother, Norbu, quite well. I visited him often at the Drepung Monastery where he lived. Later, after the Chinese invaded Lhasa, we stayed together in the south of Tibet for a month and made lots of excursions in the beautiful forests there; we even crossed the border into Bhutan.

Yapshi Tagtser, the Holy Family's house in Lhasa, was just east of the Potala. We played many sporting games there through the years. The young Dalai Lama would look down into the garden with his binoculars and telescope to see us enjoying ourselves. The boy could never join us in person, but at least he could watch his family under informal circumstances through his binoculars and in the movies I made for him.

*Seen here with his personal servant [right], the Dalai Lama's youngest brother, Ngari Rinpoche, was born shortly after we arrived in Lhasa. During the escape from the Chinese, most of his family [below] stayed in the Chumbi Valley for a month, where Norbu [left] and I made many excursions.*

## The Young Couple and the Apricot

Several months after Peter Aufschnaiter and I arrived in Lhasa, we were already well-fed and had forgotten our hardships on the road. During the period surrounding Buddha's birthday, we, like everyone else, went around the five-mile Lingkor encircling Lhasa and the Potala. These were our poorest months, but already we had everything we needed, most of which we'd received from the parents of His Holiness, the Dalai Lama.

Among the many beggars sitting along the Lingkor we saw a young couple who waved to us. We walked over and discovered they were the two people we had met two months before on a 20,000-foot pass during our escape journey. When we had seen them last, we were at the end of our strength, stumbling along the stony road across the highest pass in the world that is open all year. This young couple had suddenly caught up with us. The woman was very pretty with rosy cheeks and thick black pigtails. She was a gleam of sunshine to

us in those hard, heavy days. Once, as we were resting, she reached into the pocket of her heavy sheepskin coat and smilingly handed each of us a dried apricot. This was the most precious gift I ever received anywhere in the world.

Now here they were in Lhasa. They said that they were on pilgrimage and had made offerings in the central temple to the Jowo Rinpoche because they had committed a sin, they had run away from their homeland. Like many nomads who arrived in Lhasa, they admitted that life here was very difficult for them and they thought longingly back to the beautiful country in the Changthang, the northern plains where the nomads lived. Here in Lhasa they had to work very hard, while in the Changthang they could travel around with their herds to fresh grazing grounds. They felt they didn't have to work at all as nomads. Nature gave them everything: the hair of the yak and the sheep to make cloth for their tents, furs to dress in to keep them warm. They felt no danger in their homeland, they would never be afraid of not getting

*Nomads, pilgrims, and professional beggars collected alms along the Lingkor, the ring road that encircled Lhasa and the Potala. Here Peter Aufschnaiter and I encountered two disillusioned nomads we had first met during a difficult period on our escape.*

enough food for the next day. But in Lhasa things were different. They were surprised that they had to work for daily necessities, even if it was only a place to spend the night or a cup of tea. They felt that people in Lhasa were greedy, demanding things that in the Changthang you wouldn't think about.

So they were here on the Lingkor trying to get enough money and *tsampa* to walk back across the passes to their homeland. We invited them to our modest home, where we had lots of barley, rice, and butter, and we supplied them for their return to the Changthang, their nomadic home, where they had plenty of meat, butter, cheese, milk, and where nature could provide for all their needs.

## Reforestation

During the multiweek New Year's Festival in Lhasa, tea had to be prepared for at least 20,000 monks. The government supplied the wood and yak dung used as cooking fuel. But there was little of either fuel in the Lhasa region, so people had to travel long distances to gather enough for all the monks. After Aufschnaiter and I were settled in Lhasa for a while, one of the highest monks asked us whether we had any ideas on how to provide fuel wood for the festival. We suggested planting willow and poplar trees along the Kyichu River, where there were large bare areas covered with gravel. We had workers dig ditches two feet deep until we reached groundwater from the river, then we set twigs in the ditches and filled them up again. In some places Aufschnaiter made an additional canal for more water. Soon the twigs sprouted leaves, and two years later we could cut enough wood off these fast-growing trees to cook all the tea during the New Year's Festival. It was the first reforestation in Tibet.

The young willow planting [above] leads to a commemorative stone heap honoring a Mongolian regent who was killed here during the reign of the Sixth Dalai Lama. More willows can be seen along the Lingkor, behind a mendicant lama with a damaru [left].

## Peter Aufschnaiter

Peter Aufschnaiter was my great friend and companion throughout my years in Tibet. After escaping together from the internment camp in India, we traveled as a team for nearly two years crossing Tibet and shared a house for our first two years in Lhasa. Altogether I was with him almost fourteen years, from the beginning of the Nanga Parbat reconnaissance expedition, through prison, and then seven years in Tibet. During this whole time I couldn't have imagined a better partner. I don't think that either of us could have survived alone during our long journey to Lhasa.

Aufschnaiter was quiet and introverted, but the Tibetans could see immediately that he was a good and generous man, and they always respected and liked him very much.

Born in Kitzbühel, Austria, Aufschnaiter had studied to be an agricultural engineer. His training made him very useful to the Tibetans because nobody else in Lhasa had his engineering knowledge. Not long after our arrival, the government asked him to build a canal that would carry water to some dry fields near Lhasa. The Tibetans had tried to dig a canal, but their system did not carry the water far enough—they simply dug a trench in the earth for the water to flow in, and pretty soon the water level was below ground. So Aufschnaiter found a sixty-year-old theodolite at Tsarong's house, and used this measuring device to help in surveying for a canal with raised levies. We then built this canal, which worked perfectly. Then he advised the government on a dike to protect the Norbulingkha from flooding; I supervised the construction of this dike, which also worked flawlessly.

But the most interesting work we did together was measuring Lhasa to make a map of the city. We had become jacks-of-all-trades to the government, and they wanted us to build a sewer system. In order to do this work, we had to have an accurate map—all that existed so far were very rough drawings. We made our measurements early in the morning because once crowds filled the bazaar, it became impossible to use either our

Peter Aufschnaiter
taking measurements
from Chagpori for our
city plan of Lhasa and
environs. The three
prongs on top of the
good-luck shrine keep
birds from landing.

measuring tapes or the theodolite any longer. Curious what we were doing, people would surround us; they kept wanting to look into the instrument or into the houses we were measuring to find out what we were looking at. So we went out very early every morning with one Tibetan man to help us.

After many months of work we finally had precisely measured the city, the road to Norbulingkha, and the five-mile-long Lingkor. Inside the Norbulingkha I had to measure with the lengths of my steps instead of with a tape measure because the Regent did not approve of this work—he thought it was too modern. So our measurements there were very crude in comparison with Lhasa. A year later (our third year in Lhasa), I measured the lengths and widths of every house and large garden in the city; at the same time I collected the names of all the houses and of all the shops in the bazaar—about a thousand names in all.

After two years in Lhasa, Peter was sent to work on installing a power station. He lived for the next few years in a nice little bungalow

*Peter Aufschnaiter examining his water gauge on the Kyichu River [right]. I could see his new canal [below] from the roof of my house. One of our favorite excursions was to Tra Yerpa [left], the famous cave of Padmasambhava, the holy man who brought Buddhism to Tibet. Here Aufschnaiter is with Tsering Yangzom, stepsister of George Tsarong.*

a few miles east of town where he began work on a big dam across the Kyichu River and on a canal that would go down through Lhasa. I designed a plan for a new Lhasa that would stand on both sides of this big canal. I planned new government buildings, and most of the nobility, who were all well-to-do, planned to build new houses there. Aufschnaiter enjoyed working on the dam, but his greatest pleasure came when he was making an excavation at the dam site and discovered the first archeological finds in Tibet.

During our escape across Tibet to Lhasa, Aufschnaiter sold his watch, a Rolex that he liked very much. Some years later, a merchant in the Barkor bazaar came up to me and asked if I wanted to buy a broken watch. I looked at it closely, and it was Aufschnaiter's Rolex. So I bought it and brought it to a Mohammedan who could work on such fine machinery. He fixed the watch, and I was able to make a present of it to Aufschnaiter for his birthday; he was surprised and pleased to have it again. It was a great pleasure to bring happiness to such a wonderful man.

*Peter Aufschnaiter on a mountain excursion [left] and with a caravan [above] next to a little canal from the Kyichu River. This was one of the most beautiful spots around Lhasa, popular for picnicking. Water spirits were said to live here.*

## The Dike

Every summer when the remnants of the Indian monsoon came to Lhasa, the Kyichu River spilled over its banks and threatened to flood the Norbulingkha. So the Tibetan government asked Aufschnaiter and me whether we could build a better dike than theirs. To build their own, the Tibetans carried tens of thousands of stones from long distances and piled them vertically along the river's edge. Their dike was around ten feet thick; but when the monsoon came, the lower stones would wash out and the whole thing would collapse. Every year the same thing happened.

So Aufschnaiter designed a one-mile dike that sloped toward the river. We built up a big wall of soil, and, on the river side of the wall, we put stones—but only one stone deep. The idea was that the water would slip along this slanted wall and not wash away the lower stones as it had with the vertical wall. This was the standard technique for dike-building all over the world, but the Tibetans

couldn't believe it. They said that if their thousands of stones didn't hold, how could a single-thickness layer on an earth embankment ever last?

I supervised the construction, which began early in the summer. In the Tibetan system, bringing the stones was a form of taxation paid by the population. But it was difficult to get enough workers, and we were in a hurry to build the dike before the monsoon arrived. So I suggested that I could get workers if I paid them, like in Europe. At the end of each work day, a laborer would get one silver *tranka*. In addition, I insisted the workers get tea twice during the day and soup at the end of the day. With this system, it was no problem to get 700 or so laborers.

Maybe ninety percent were women, because nearly one-fifth of the Tibetan men were in monasteries and there was always a surplus of women. They were not very strong, but they aided themselves by attaching ropes to the shovel. One woman would guide the shovel's handle and one or two others would pull on the ropes, thus forcing the shovel into

*The Kyichu River
flowed past Lhasa
(Lhasa is in the center
of the photo, the Potala
to its left). Each year
floods threatened the
Norbulingkha.*

The new dike
[above] protected the
Norbulingkha perfectly,
much to the surprise
and delight of the
cabinet ministers on
their inspection tour
[far right]. The dike's
design was new, as
was the concept of
paying laborers [right]
for their work.

the ground. They carried earth and stones in baskets on their heads.

Every day had its distractions. Over and over worms would be dug up. Since Tibetans never kill, the women would scream and carry the worms to safety. Also, paying for this kind of work was an entirely new concept. After several days of earning a *tranka* each day, fewer and fewer workers came back: They couldn't see any point in continuing to labor when they already had enough money for the next several weeks. It became a big problem.

Finally, as the monsoon approached, we recruited beggars. But the same thing happened with them—after two or three days of pay, they would go sit down on the Barkor, turn the prayer wheel, and collect alms. So I finally used some of the Dalai Lama's 500 bodyguards to finish the work, just in time.

All four cabinet ministers came on an official inspection once the work was done. They and other officers went out in yak-hide boats as Aufschnaiter and I explained how the new dike worked. It was an unforgettable day for me. The dike didn't wash out, and I became very proud of it.

## Farmers

The Tibetans had careful systems for tilling their fields, rotating crops so the fields could recover. In the south, in Kyirong, the fields had a cycle of seven years. Usually the farmers would plow the fields with yaks, but sometimes they worked all day with primitive spades. After turning the earth in the fall, they flooded the fields with water. The water froze and prevented erosion by the sandstorms.

The typical farmer's home had a flat roof with prayer flags at the corners. There was also lots of thornwood and dried dung on the roof, both of which were being kept for cooking in the winter. During the cloudless winter months people would sit on the roof in the warm sun and spin wool or knit.

After harvest, the farmers often threshed the grain with a flail. Other times the bundles were just spread out on the ground and

*You can see the Potala [above] behind this woman threshing barley at the eastern outskirts of Lhasa. Cats, like the one to her right, were very rare; dogs were the common animal. A few miles east of Lhasa, near where Peter Aufschnaiter lived, farmers tilled their fields with spades [right]. In the background is a typical farmer's house with its prayer flags.*

animals like yaks and donkeys walked on it in a circle until the grain had come out. The yaks didn't always want to do this, but they liked to hear singing, so the farmers would sing to them. In the afternoon when the wind always came up, the farmers would throw the threshings up into the air so the wind could separate the remainder of the chaff from the grain.

## Games and Gambling

Whether commoners or noblemen, Tibetans loved to gamble. The most popular game was called *sho* and involved a wooden bowl in which two dice were rolled. Everyone played the game, even people like Tsipön Lukhang, Tibet's auditor general, who was well known for not gambling. The wealthy people in Lhasa played many other games, but among the populace, *sho* was played with especially great passion.

On the big caravans carrying wool to India or crossing central Asia to China, Tibetans wore large *lok-pa*, sheepskin furs. Above the belt they had a large pocket called an *ambag* in which they transported nearly everything they needed for daily life, including *tsampa*, butter, and bowls. But most importantly, nearly everybody carried the game of *sho* in his *ambag*. While on a caravan, which could last for months or even years, people would sit down after unloading for the night, make a wall with the goods to protect them against wind and storms, cook their tea, and play *sho* for hours on end. They slipped off the right sleeve of their fur coats and with the bare right shoulder and arm, they let out a loud scream as they threw the dice onto a round leather pillow. The game often led to quarrels, which could grow rough, especially when the players had too much *chang*, the Tibetan barley beer.

Another game better reflected the light-hearted side of Tibetans. Using a diagram-*thangka*, two people would throw a pair of dice, which instead of dots had the holy words *om mani padme hum* , "hail the jewel in the lotus flower." The winner was the one who first reached nirvana on the *thangka*.

The wealthier citizens of Tibet played yet another game, *mah-jong*, which was imported from China. In the night when you walked or rode through the narrow streets of Lhasa, you could hear through the windows the clinking sounds of ivory "stones." People played the whole night through—often with lots of money at stake.

Women played a game called *bagchen*, which also involved ivory stones. They usually sat

*Playing* sho, *the Tibetan national passion. The swastika on the wall is a Tibetan good luck sign that has been used for thousands of years, directed left or right depending on which religious school it was related to.*

Even monks weren't
above cheating [above],
as evidenced by the one
sneaking a glance at my
friend Wangdü's cards
in this game. Women
and men typically
gambled at separate
tables [right].

separately from the men, and men and women rarely gambled together. And there were games using Tibetan cards, round cards from India, and for bridge, European cards.

There is one more game, called *mig mag*, that played a big part in Tibetan culture. *Mig mag* translates as "the war of many eyes." The game requires great intelligence; it is as difficult as chess. In Lhasa the most famous players were the Mongol *geshe*s, monks who taught in the big monastery of Drepung. Other famed players included some high Tibetan nobility like the cabinet ministers Surkhang and Ragashar. These noblemen would send their horses five miles to the Drepung Monastery to fetch a *geshe* to play in Lhasa and stay overnight. Normally monks

were not allowed to gamble, but *mig mag* was not as severely prohibited. *Sho* was definitely forbidden to monks. Once, when I photographed monks secretly playing the game, they requested that I not show the picture to anyone because they were afraid that the Regent would punish them. When Tibetans played *mig mag* against the highly educated Mongol *geshe*s, they were always surrounded by onlookers—like we see in Europe around chess players.

I personally never played any of these games for money and often tried to get the Tibetans away from their gambling. When I introduced many of my friends to sports, it was partly in an effort to divert them from this Tibetan obsession with gambling.

## Sports

*The Tibetans called skating "walking on knives." It was my favorite sport in Lhasa and attracted a lot of attention. This quiet branch of the Kyichu River was located below Chagpori.*

Some Western sports had been introduced to Tibet during the time of the reform-minded Thirteenth Dalai Lama; there had even been a Lhasa soccer team. But the monks didn't like "foreign" behavior like soccer-playing. Perhaps they were afraid of losing power. So when the British started a school in Lhasa and engaged a soccer coach, the monks eventually drove him out. After the deaths of the Thirteenth Dalai Lama and the liberal regent who succeeded him, the strict Tagdra Regent came to power and even forbade soccer-playing. Still, I thought introducing sports to my Lhasa friends might divert them from doing so much gambling.

We started our athletics quietly, without teams and trying not to attract attention. We would go to the river, where I taught some of my friends to swim, and in winter we even started skating. To the southwest of Chagpori was a branch of the Kyichu River where the water froze the earliest. It was not very deep there, which made it safer in case the ice broke.

For skates, I screwed some old blades I found—left by a British trade mission—onto U.S. Army surplus boots.

At the beginning of our stay in Lhasa, the British tried to have Peter Aufschnaiter and me forced out of Tibet, but eventually they gave up and the British and we became great friends. Later on I even built a tennis court within the British Mission's compound, which was located just below and west of Chagpori. I spread very fine gravel and flattened it, then spread yak dung on top of this. The dung worked like glue on the gravel, giving us a very good surface.

Gatherings at the tennis court with the British, and later on with the Indians, became social events. We played tennis at least once a week, and in the evening we played bridge and enjoyed European dinners (the British Mission had an Indian cook who knew how to make European food). The gatherings soon became popular with all the foreigners. The ambassador of Nepal, a round little fellow, was very agile and fast. He was one of our best tennis players. And the Chinese secretary to the ambassador also enjoyed tennis with us. And of course I brought some of my Tibetan friends to play. Wangdü, the

*Tennis became popular after I built a court out of yak dung [left]. We played many other sports in the gardens belonging to the Dalai Lama's parents [right]. The table-tennis-playing nobleman on the left [below] was the Dalai Lama's chief chamberlain.*

*Traditional Tibetan
sports included shooting
arrows for distance
[right] and at targets
while galloping a horse.
At ceremonies [above]
they used special
arrowheads that made
a whistling noise.*

Tsedrung monk was especially interested and would also have liked to play soccer. The best tennis player was the British Mission's leader, Hugh Richardson.

Tennis, swimming, and skating became so popular that we started doing more and more sports, and with the children I started additional games, like the blanket toss. The Dalai Lama's family grew very interested in these activities, and soon we erected a tent in his parents' garden and played various sports there over several days while being fed by their cooks and our own, whom we brought from home. These were unforgettably beautiful times.

The new activities gradually became known around Lhasa, especially skating, which the Tibetans called "walking on knives." We often had spectators by the frozen river. One day the Dalai Lama asked his brother Lobsang to have me make movies of our skating. Showing him these movies became my first meeting with His Holiness, who was only fourteen at that time. I told him that even the ancient Romans and Greeks found

sport an important part of life—and of running a government.

Of course I had to proceed slowly and carefully so as not to offend the ruling monks. But eventually, I had one big advantage, and that was that I had become a friend of His Holiness. Everyone in town knew that "Henrig"—that was what they called me—was taking pictures of these sports for His Holiness.

Of course there were also traditional Tibetan sports. They did archery at targets and for distance. They also shot at targets while riding full speed on horseback, firing first with their old muzzleloading guns, then changing as quickly as possible in order to hit the next target with an arrow. And there were whistling arrows, where the arrowhead was a little wooden case with holes; when the arrow flew through the air it made lovely whistling noises. They also had wrestling, weightlifting using stones, and horse racing. They even raced horses without riders, with people shouting at the horses to make them go faster.

The Dob-Dob, those monk policemen who looked so fierce during the big ceremo-

*Swimming was not very popular in Tibet, in part because the water was very cold. Here we are at the Kyichu River.*

nies, were well known for their own sports. They knew that I liked athletics, so they invited me after one of the ceremonies to come do some with them. Having heard of our jumping achievements in the West, they said they would show me that they could jump twice as far as we could. There was an open space below Drepung Monastery where they had set up a kind of springboard, and down the slope was some sand. They jumped from this board and flew downhill through the air for at least thirty-five to forty feet. It was spectacularly impressive seeing them flying through the air with their robes billowing about.

I was rather reluctant to do it myself, but I had to participate. Jumping barefoot on the rough surface, I covered maybe half their distance. They also had foot races. One day I was racing them uphill and I somehow got into the lead. The winner had to touch a stone first, and just before I reached it a competing monk held me by my belt and passed me. There was an enormous roar of joy that the Tibetan had beaten me.

## Washing

During spring and summer, you could often see women washing clothes on the banks of the Kyichu River. The standard laundry practice involved stamping the garments with your feet or beating them against stones. Some women used soap, but mostly they used borax, which was plentiful in the highlands. Spring was the season to clean the fur coats and lambskin trousers worn in winter. They would pour wet sand on the fur side of the skins; when the sand dried, they would beat it out of the fur with sticks, singing all the while. The garment turned fluffy and fresh again. In Tibet's cold winters, fur was essential daily clothing, and it was always worn in the warmest fashion, which is with the fur on the inside against your naked skin. The Tibetans asked me again and again, "Why do your women in the West wear the fur on the outside?"

Most books on Tibet describe Tibetans as dirty and unwashed. But one must understand it is bitterly cold in the winter through-

out Tibet, especially in Lhasa, and there was no heating. Water had to be warmed on a yak-dung fire. All this made washing difficult and unpopular. It was also less necessary to wash in Tibet, because there was practically no decay—or foul odors—in the cold, dry, high-altitude air.

Since they had no running water in Lhasa, residents had a special system for washing their hands, using a ladle. They would put the ladle between their teeth, or squeeze it between chin and shoulder, and bend forward, dribbling water on both hands. The well-to-do would have their servants pour the water. One day a Tibetan told me, "We Tibetans are actually cleaner than you because you wash yourself in your own dirt." He meant that I used a washing bowl, scrubbing my hands in the water without replacing it, while the Tibetans used continuously fresh water pouring out of the ladle.

To wash their hair, Tibetan women used a coarse soap, borax, or a bark extract, then put a lot of butter in their hair and made braids. One day when I passed a woman

*After playing tennis
and other sports, we
cleaned up under a
makeshift shower—a
jerry can filled with
water heated on a
yak-dung fire.*

To wash clothes along
the banks of the
Kyichu River [above],
women would stamp
the garments with their
feet or beat them
against stones. Hands
were washed [right]
under continuously
running water
from a ladle.

washing her hair and upper body I asked, "Why don't you wash yourself further down?" She looked very astonished, and said, "*Dende a yö?*," meaning, "Does anyone do that?"

After I introduced some sports like tennis to my friends in Lhasa, we had to think about cleaning the sweat off. So I built a shower, filling a jerry can from India (from surplus American stuff) with lukewarm water and suspending it from a tree in the garden. I then unscrewed the lid slightly, allowing the water to trickle down. This makeshift shower became very popular. The water we used was always a little brownish because it had to be heated on a yak-dung fire. The smell of the dung penetrated the water. When you entered a tent or a home in Tibet there was always a mixture of the smell of butter tea (mostly rancid), sweat, and smoke. But after you lived there you got used to this smell and eventually you came to enjoy its pervasiveness.

## Yak-hide Boats

Professional boatmen owned coracles made of yak hides stretched over wooden frames. The boatmen were organized into a guild, and were all earnest, proud, and extremely strong. After floating downriver they had to carry their heavy boats—about 200 pounds each when wet, and maybe 150 pounds dry—back upstream on their shoulders. Sometimes they hiked back following the shoreline, but it was often more direct to cross over high passes instead of tracing the bends in the river. These men typically had one or two sheep who floated downstream with them, and when the men carried their boats upriver, the sheep carried little loads on their own backs. These loads weighed about twenty pounds and included blankets, cooking utensils for tea, and barley flour. It was touching to meet a boatman high in the mountains with a loaded sheep following him without a leash.

Lobsang, Jigme, Wangdü, and other friends and I would often cross the Kyichu

*When we tried to race with coracles on our backs [right], we discovered just how strong the boatmen [left] had to be. Wet, a coracle weighs about 200 pounds. In the middle of the photo at right is my great friend, Wangdü.*

River near Lhasa because we usually went on excursions on the other side of the river. We always had great fun together as I tried to distract them from gambling by introducing them to alternatives like hiking. One of the hardest things we ever did was to carry a boatman's coracle in the thin high-altitude air. The boats are carried on the shoulders using one paddle laid cross-ways as a yoke, while the second paddle is lashed below. Once we tried to race each other with these boats on our backs, but we could only carry them for about sixty feet. This taught us how strong the boatmen had to be.

*A boatman [right] will row our party across the Kyichu River [above] on one of our many excursions. Lobsang is the one wearing glasses, Jigme is left of him and Wangdü at far left.*

## Yar-so

One of the most colorful events during the multiweek New Year's festivities occurred on the twenty-second day of the first month of the year. Called Yar-so, the occasion honored two young men of high nobility. They had to be very rich to accept this honor, because they had to pay for the ceremonies themselves. Still, it was almost impossible to refuse the appointment, bestowed by the government on a rotating basis to the noble families.

One of my closest friends became a Yar-so "general" during the time I was in Lhasa: the young D. N. Tsarong, called George, in whose house I lived during most of my first two years in Lhasa. His father was the legendary Tsarong Sawang Chenpo, who had become the "bright eye," or the favorite, of the Thirteenth Dalai Lama after defending the ruler during his escape from the Chinese in 1910. Soon Tsarong, who was born a commoner, became one of the highest ministers in the Tibetan government. His son took the name "George" while

The two Yar-so
"generals" stand before
the master of ceremony.
When the Shenyen puts
his fifteen-foot pole
upright, it means the
Yar-sos must prostrate
themselves in front of
the Tsuglagkhang,
where the Dalai
Lama is upstairs.

Wearing fine clothing
and borrowed jewelry,
the "chang-girls"
[left] served the
Yar-so ceremony.
After a stage in the
Barkor, the Yar-so
"generals," including
George Tsarong [right],
rode out to the Trabchi
plain [below] for
sporting games.

*In big fur hats imported from Europe and old czarist-Russian brocade garments, the Yar-so "generals" [right] enjoy festivities in their honor. Chang bowls sit before them. George Tsarong [above] is flanked by his "officers," all noblemen.*

attending St. Joseph's College in Darjeeling.

The entire Yar-so ceremony proved fascinating. The two "generals" and their attendants all dressed in expensive old brocades from czarist Russia. George wore a blue fox hat imported from Europe. Everyone drank lots of *chang*, the Tibetan barley beer, and the "*chang*-girls" who served it wore the most expensive jewelry and the most elaborate head ornaments in Tibet. It wasn't their own jewelry but was borrowed from various important families. There were six of these women, two of whom were well known for their knowledge of ceremonies. They were employed at all the big events, including marriages and births.

On the day of the Yar-so, George rode into town from his house on the outskirts of Lhasa. Along the way, he met the second "general," a young man from the famous house of Sampho, a family whose ancestors included a former Dalai Lama. They continued together to the Bharkor, the ring road in the center of Lhasa, where two thrones had been erected under umbrellas. People flocked around, bringing presents to the two Yar-sos and throwing them *khatags*, which piled up by their thrones.

After an hour or so they walked to the Tsuglagkhang Temple, the holiest of all holy places in Lhasa. Later they rode in procession to the Trabchi plain behind the Potala, accompanied by several hundred soldiers dressed up in old armor. The day-long Yar-so ceremony finished up at Yapshi Lhalu, a noble family's house just north of the Potala, where there were a number of large tents covered with good-luck embroidery. Here they played sporting games, like archery, gun shooting, and horse racing, both bareback and with saddles. All the while, so much *chang* flowed that most of the cavalrymen could barely keep themselves upright on their horses. With the Tibetans' love of pomp and fancy clothes, the whole population of Lhasa loved Yar-so, even those who could only watch.

## Mocking

The Tibetans have always had a sense of humor. In their gaiety, they would poke fun at almost everyone. Even the highest officials, like the Regent, and the most sacred, like the State Oracle, would be mocked. Only the Dalai Lama was spared this treatment.

They also love to gossip, and since there were no newspapers, their favorite way to communicate was with a form of street song. Usually these songs had political themes pointed against the established aristocracy. People especially loved to criticize the newly rich who had risen through bribery. After the death of a Dalai Lama there was always a time of turmoil when the large monasteries vied for power and the big families struggled to rise and place a family member as a cabinet minister. This was an especially fertile time for gossip and mocking street songs.

The lyrics of these songs, which were full of rude sarcasm and irony, were set to old, established melodies. Officially the song's

*The younger brother of Phala Dronyer Chemo, the Dalai Lama's chief chamberlain [above], enjoyed mocking the history-plays performed in the Norbulingkha. Though the State Oracle was highly respected, Tibetans could still have fun by imitating him in trance [right].*

author remained anonymous, though one could often guess from the text the clever person behind it. Even though his name might be whispered, the author was never punished. Pretty young girls walking in groups through the Barkor would sing these songs, as would workers swinging their shovels while helping us on the dike. None feared any consequences because it was all great fun for the Tibetans.

## The Potala and Buddha's Birthday

The name "Potala" is not Tibetan, it's Sanskrit, and refers to a mythical mountain on the southern point of the Indian continent. Tibetans usually call the great building above Lhasa "Tse," which means "summit." By any name, this is one of the most impressive and beautiful buildings in the world, and for 300 years it was the seat of the royal as well as the religious head of Tibet: the Dalai Lama.

Thirteen stories tall, the Potala is said to have more than 1,000 rooms, which I think is an exaggeration—but it would still be a hopeless enterprise to try to visit every room. There were treasury chambers which required double keys kept by special high officials—even some which only the Dalai Lama could open. Then there were deep, dark dungeonlike rooms where there was no daylight at all. The Potala's interior was gloomy and oppressive—a terrible contrast to its fantastically beautiful exterior.

This massive structure was built on

The Potala, seen here
from just outside the
Western Gate, was
built 300 years ago by
the Fifth Dalai Lama.
A fortress used by
former kings of Tibet
had stood for centuries
on the same site before
being destroyed by
raiding Mongols.

*A gate [left] led from
the Lingkor to the
anchorage for the yak-
hide coracles used during
the celebration of
Buddha's birthday. Even
the ministers [below]
came to enjoy the
beautiful surroundings
on this festive day.*

Mapori, "Red Mountain," by the Fifth Dalai Lama in the seventeenth century. The building was not actually completed during the Dalai Lama's lifetime, but the regent withheld news of his death for ten years so the construction could be finished—he was afraid the workers would not complete their difficult task if they knew His Holiness had died.

Those laborers now have an unlikely monument to their efforts: a beautiful lake. Because the Tibetans had no cement, they mortared with clay instead, which they dug for the Potala from an ever-growing pit on the north side of Mapori. A little creek flowed there, and, eventually, the creek filled the cavity, creating a lake. In the middle of this lake was a little island on which a temple was built and named Dzongyab Lukhang, the "House of the Serpent."

On the fifteenth of the fourth Tibetan month—the month when Buddha was born—thousands of people would flock to this lake, where the steep walls of the Potala reflected in green water. Wearing their finest clothing, they would picnic in the shade of willow trees and make offerings at the temple.

Dozens of boatmen would have brought their yak-hide coracles there the day before and camped around the lake. On the fifteenth they would be busy giving rides to joyous picnickers bringing khatags to the Lukhang and throwing tsampa into the air while shouting, "So-so, so-so!" This would go on all day long.

The nicest event came after people had drunk plenty of chang, Tibetan barley beer. Wooden planks would then be brought out and lashed to the rims of coracles, whereupon the revelers would dance, with their feet making wonderful sounds on these boards, loud and rhythmic. My friend Wangdü was especially good at dancing and even put on great shows with Western step-dances. He was very popular with the unmarried girls, for whom Buddha's birthday was always a great occasion to dress and flirt, drink and dance. Of course these platforms lashed to the coracles were not very safe, especially after dancers had been drinking, and sometimes the less skillful would plunge into the water. When this happened, all the picnickers would howl endlessly with laughter.

Buddha's birthday
was an occasion to
dress in fine clothes
and have fun. Boats
[right] took revelers to
a temple in the middle
of a lake on the
verdant north side of
the Potala [above].

## Butter Tea

It was said that Tibetans drank a hundred cups of tea a day, but that certainly was not true. The legend probably started because every time wealthy Tibetans sipped from their teacups, servants would add fresh tea. This they did perhaps fifty or sixty times, but the person drinking never actually finished any single cupful.

There was another legend about tea, and this was that Tibetans loved *rancid* butter tea. True, Tibet's most popular drink, butter tea, was usually made with rancid butter. But most Lhasa residents, even the wealthy ones, didn't have the option to use fresh butter. The female yak, sometimes called the *dri*, lived in the mountains far from Lhasa and wouldn't give more than one or two quarts of milk a day. When a farmer started making butter out of this small amount of milk, he could only get a tiny bit. Then he put this into a leather bag, usually made of yak hide. Strangely enough, the hairy side of the skin faced inside (smaller quantities of butter were stored in sheep,

goat, or yak stomachs and bladders). Every now and then the farmer pushed a little piece of butter into the bag, and every time he did this a lot of oxygen came between the layers of old and fresh butter. So it started getting rancid at the very beginning. Since the farmer only had two or three cows, it took him weeks, maybe months to fill up a ninety-pound load of butter. Once the bag was finally filled, the farmer sewed it up and the butter began its journey toward Lhasa.

Travel from southern or western Tibet to Lhasa involved several hundred miles of travel by yak caravan. The yak—this headstrong, stubborn oxen who was the most precious animal in Tibet—walks very slowly, at best two miles per hour. Since the yaks weren't fed, they had to graze as they walked and during rest breaks. After four or five hours of travel, the caravan stopped and the caravan drivers used the yak loads to build a small fortress against the wind while the yaks grazed for the rest of the day. Weeks or months passed like this before the caravan reached Lhasa and the loads of butter were put into

*To make the Tibetan national drink, this young man churns butter and tea. The emulsion replenishes the body's salt, fat, and water—all vital nutrients in Tibet's cold, dry climate.*

*Noblemen and women*
*socialize with tea in*
*front of the Kumbum*
*monument in Gyangtse*
*[above]. The girl*
*[right] sits behind three*
*fancy teacups, complete*
*with stands and covers.*

vast government warehouses awaiting further distribution. Sometimes a year or two could go by from when the cow was milked until the butter was consumed, and it would be hard to imagine it *not* being rancid after all that time. But I never got used to the green or yellowish surface film on the tea and I found the smell nearly nauseating. It didn't help that hair scraped off the inside of the bag often swam on top of the tea. I would usually blow back the floating fat so I could drink only the tea underneath.

Before pouring the tea, the server always turned the teapot several times in a circle in order to mix the butter into the tea. Then he put a cover on your drinking bowl. You couldn't drink right away, but had to leave your tea standing for several minutes instead. Then the server asked you to drink it. I never knew why you weren't supposed to drink immediately; maybe it was to give the butter time to float to the surface to prove that the host used a lot of butter and was not stingy with his guests.

Later on we sometimes got fresh butter in Lhasa and I found that butter tea is really the very best drink you can have at this altitude. In the thin, dry air you lose water all the time; at the same time, of course, you lose a lot of salt. Even when you perspire you don't see any sweat, but suddenly you notice you have salt on your forehead. The Tibetan

drink provides salt and liquid. The tea gives you stamina, and you get vitamins, nourishment, and calories from the butter.

During the festivals—and in fact every day at the large monasteries—it was a big production to get tea to all the thousands of monks. One after the other, in single file, the cooks' assistants ran out of the kitchen carrying large containers of tea. Whole groups of ten or twelve were running around to satisfy the monks.

These cooks' assistants were incredibly dirty; their coats were shiny with butter and they had a fantastic smell—a mixture of rancid butter, tea, sweat, dirt, and smoke. I had not planned to take a picture of them because I was afraid they might have felt offended and they were known for being aggressive, like the Dob-Dobs. But I made a joke: I asked them how often they bathed. This made them roar with laughter, because they never washed themselves. Then they asked me to take their picture.

Wearing clothes shiny
with butter, these cooks'
assistants carried tea for
thousands of monks
during the New Year's
festival. They roared with
laughter when I asked if
they ever washed. The
Dalai Lama's cooks
[left] are wearing their
traditional chef's hats.
Did Western chefs take
fashion tips from the
Tibetans?

## The Market

The big market in Lhasa centered on the inner circle in the city, the Barkor, which was bordered by the houses of the well-to-do nobility and the central temple, the Tsuglagkhang. In this bazaar you could find nearly anything you could imagine, from used sheepskin clothing to Thermos bottles. When people died or moved, nearly all of their possessions would be for sale, even precious religious objects. Many of the most popular goods were imported from India, including aluminum pots, which were cheap, light, and easy to transport because you could stack different sizes inside each other. Tea was, of course, the most important thing sold. Many cups were drunk every day, and in the market you could find bricks and balls of tea from all over Asia.

Since the sun was so strong in the dry air and high altitude, many vendors in the open area of the Barkor had peculiar awnings to provide shade. These perched on a single pole and you could direct the cloth umbrella

*The straw market [above] was slightly east of Lhasa. In the background is the Gyalhakhang, the Mohammedan mosque. This scene in the Barkor [right] shows the crowding typical of the market. The Ping, or pea-flour noodles, were extremely popular in Lhasa. On the right side is sliced cabbage; it's not quite sauerkraut, but similar.*

There were two kinds of
tea, bricks and round
balls. The bricks usually
came from China, while
the round balls came
from Assam or from
Darjeeling, India. Just
above the girl bending
down [left] is a churner
for making butter tea.
The carpets next to her
are small, as was
typical for Lhasa.

*Behind the upstairs curtains of the Tsuglagkhang [above, right side of picture] was the Foreign Office, where I reported while working for the government. The aluminum pots in the foreground were a popular item imported from India. Tibetan women's boots [left] were beautifully embroidered with ornaments and flowers.*

toward the sun, so you were always protected. Tibetans always loved to trade, and the bazaar was typically an excited, crowded place.

My friends in Lhasa advised me that I should start trading in something because my salary was not very high. I said, "I don't know what I would trade in," to which they replied, "Well, for us here in Tibet, the number-one business is buying and selling tea. Sometimes you find the price is lower on one end of the bazaar than on the other. So you buy a load at the low end and sell it on the other for a little profit without actually needing cash; like this you make your money." I told them that in Europe I wouldn't know what I would trade. They said, "You must trade in something you in the West use every day. You shave yourself every day, so trade in razor blades."

125

## Butchers and Blacksmiths

Because life was sacred to Tibetan Buddhists, butchers were treated as outcasts from society and had to live outside the city limits. Typically, the butchers were Mohammedans from countries neighboring Tibet. In Lhasa they used to live behind a wall constructed with animal bones and yak horns, and even built their houses with these skeletal remains. Later they built regular houses.

These people, called *ragyapa*, were very important in Lhasa because they removed dead animals from the streets—most commonly horses and dogs. They knew themselves to be irreplaceable, and they were proud of their jobs, which were handed down through the generations. From time to time these *ragyapa* went to all the houses in Lhasa and begged for alms. They were quite successful, in part because people knew they were important to the city. But they also used a form of blackmail in their begging: If they didn't get what they expected, they might get wild and aggressive, yelling vile expressions at the stingy household. They might even put a curse on the house. So everybody right away gave enough to keep from being cursed.

When he had to kill a yak, the butcher would bind its feet with a leather strap, then throw it onto its side and harness it further. He then opened the yak's belly with a knife, and with his hand he reached inside the body to tear the artery from the heart. The animal died very quickly, and the precious blood stayed inside the body and could be used afterwards.

Because the Tibetans thought blacksmiths hurt horses when they put horseshoes on them, the blacksmiths were often treated the same as butchers. In the smaller villages, a butcher might even double as a blacksmith. When Peter Aufschnaiter and I were in Kyirong during our escape to Lhasa, we had to have our yak killed by a local blacksmith

*These Mohammedan butchers, who are about to slaughter a yak, know their profession elicits revulsion among the Buddhist population of Tibet. That's why they look apprehensive.*

*Beyond the low wall constructed with yak horns and animal bones [above] lived the butchers and the ragyapas who disposed of dead people and animals in Lhasa. Ragyapas [left] occasionally went around the city begging for alms. If they didn't get enough they might put a curse on the offending house. Here they wear round government-officer hats, which they found in the trash.*

who was also a butcher. Later we decided to ski on the neighboring glaciers, which had never been done before. Without telling my friend, I quietly found a forest with large birch trees. I cut a large log with an ax borrowed from a farmer and started making the skis. The blacksmith who had killed our yak made the ski bindings out of a piece of iron. Aufschnaiter was surprised by the primitive skis I'd made, and we had a wonderful time on the glaciers. Finally the Tibetans told us not to "ride on snow" anymore because they were afraid we might offend the spirits in the mountain and the spirits would then destroy the season's harvest.

## Prostrating

During Saga Dawa—the fourth month—everybody from Lhasa and thousands of pilgrims from elsewhere went around the Lingkor, the five-mile-long holy path encircling Lhasa and the Potala. The most pious would prostrate themselves over and over again, measuring the entire distance with the width of their bodies as they kept their heads always facing the holy sites. To protect themselves against the stony path, they wore gloves made of wood and leather, sometimes reinforced with metal, and a large, heavy apron made of sheepskin.

There was considerable ritual to their movements: As they stood up, they raised their arms, folded their hands in a praying position, and touched their foreheads with their hands. They then knelt and prostrated, stretching their arms forward as far as possible. There they placed a mark, perhaps a shell or a rare stone like an ammonite, and touched the ground with their foreheads. Sometimes you would meet some-

Pious pilgrims who prostrated around the Lingkor [above] and lived on alms [left], wore special gloves and aprons because of the rocky ground. Prostrating was strenuous work, necessitating occasional breaks for tea [far left].

one with a bump, even a bulge like a little horn, on the forehead from touching the ground so often. Prostration could be painful on the rough, stony, dusty pilgrim paths, and those who did it earned considerable respect. Some people prostrated in a hurry, not touching the ground with their foreheads. They moved much faster but did not earn as much respect for their achievements.

Prostrations were done mostly by illiterate people as compensation for not being able to read the holy scripts; they intended these acts of devotion to give them an advantage in the next rebirth. But sometimes the educated and even the nobility would prostrate along the Lingkor. The Dalai Lama's eldest sister, Tsering Drölma, though physically unfit and rather heavy, prostrated all the way around. It took her five days (two would be considered a very fast time), and she was accompanied by a servant, who also prostrated. At the end of each day they placed a little stone cairn where they had finished and went home. She was deservedly proud of her accomplishment.

The most extreme acts of prostration took years or even a lifetime. Pilgrims might prostrate in body-lengths from Lhasa to the holy mountain of Kailas, a distance of several hundred miles. They would then prostrate in body-widths around Kailas, facing the mountain the whole time. This alone took a month. And then they would prostrate back to Lhasa, and go around the holy city again. All the while, they lived on alms. During our escape through west Tibet, we encountered many of these pilgrims, of both sexes. We pretended to be on pilgrimage ourselves and often exchanged a sewing needle or a coin for some of their *tsampa*. We always parted in good spirits, having helped each other.

These prostrating pilgrims were very much respected and were all considered religious. Nomads and farmers welcomed them into their tents and houses. They were even invited to sleep in the little chapel room found in every house. If pilgrims could read, they were asked to stay and read holy books to the illiterate householders.

In Lhasa people prostrated not only along the Lingkor, but also along the shorter

Barkor, the inner holy path. All year round, pilgrims and locals prostrated in front of the Tsuglagkhang, the central temple in the heart of the city. The stone slabs in front of the temple had been polished to a shine by full-body contact over hundreds of years. I myself prostrated once before the Tsuglagkhang with two of my friends. We borrowed felt-padded gloves, and I did it for the exercise. That's when I noticed what hard work it is to make these repeated prostrations in the rarefied air.

*The especially pious would cover the entire five-mile Lingkor with body-width prostrations, facing the Potala the whole way. Such commitment earned them considerable respect.*

## Lama Mani

**M**endicant travelers called *lama mani* showed up wherever pilgrims came in great numbers. They brought with them two or three special *thangka*s that had often been handed down from generation to generation. Each of these painted scrolls told the life story of a saint or holy man. Among the most popular figures depicted were Milarepa, the famous twelfth-century poet and yogi, and Padmasambhava, the founder of Lamaism in Tibet.

The *lama mani* would point to a sequence of illustrations as he or she sang the saint's story: where he was born, that he was poor, ran away from home, lived in a cave performing miracles, became a guru, attracted many followers, and so on. One story might take a half hour of monotonous singing. But the stories were usually touching and the people who stood around listening then gave offerings of money or food. The *lama mani* served a useful function, as most Tibetans could not read. Prayer wheels were valuable for the same

The lama mani
[above] uses a stick to
point to figures in his
thangka as he sings
the life story of a holy
man. The woman's face
[left] is probably
scarred by leprosy.

reason. Learned monks, who could read, had no need for either.

These *thangka*s were an inherited form of livelihood, which made them rare and precious. The paint used natural colors from herbs, seeds, bark, ground minerals, and semiprecious stones like lapis lazuli and turquoise. To preserve these delicate colors, silk curtains covered the *thangka* when it wasn't in use and when it was rolled up for transport to the next big festival.

Most *lama mani* wandered from festival to festival, always knowing exactly where to find large groups of pilgrims who would give them alms. Some, however, preferred to sit around in Lhasa where there were many pilgrims all year round.

*These* lama mani *have set up little altars with burning butter lamps, charm boxes with personal protective deities, and bowls for alms. Above each* thangka *is a silk curtain used to protect the paint when the scroll is rolled up for transport.*

## Criminals

Criminals often showed up to beg for alms along the Lingkor, especially during the big festivals when many pilgrims came to town. These convicts were usually chained together at the hands, and had iron bars or chains between their feet to keep them from running far from the prison in the village of Shö, below the Potala. Tsarong, my host during my early time in Lhasa, told me that he once saw prisoners whom he had sentenced wearing just their hand-chains without the anklebar; he scolded them and they quickly went to get the bar. But once Tsarong had passed by, they took it off again. He laughed, ending his story, "*nying je,*" "I pity them." Though punishment wasn't typically severe, some criminals were flogged, which was painful enough, especially when they had committed a heavy crime. In that case the criminal would be flogged until the sinews in the back of his knees had been cut

*Chained together at one hand and with a bar or chain between their ankles, prisoners could beg along the Lingkor during the festivals. I don't know what these young prisoners did to get chained like this.*

and he was crippled. After this, he usually didn't stay much longer in prison; instead he would be sent to be looked after by his relatives or he would go begging. At one time penalties for major crimes, such as stealing from a religious site, included cutting off a hand and sticking the stump in boiling butter. This practice was abolished by one of the former Dalai Lamas. For a Tibetan, the worst punishment was to be kicked out of Tibet, or even just out of your home town. In the traditional method, the offender was forced to ride on a yak bull sitting backward, facing the tail. The Thirteenth Dalai Lama abolished this practice.

## New Year's Eve Festival

The big New Year's Festival lasted for several weeks, but before it could begin there was a special ceremony to destroy all the bad things from the old year. That ceremony took place on the twenty-ninth day of the twelfth month of the Tibetan calendar. In the early morning, everyone walked up the stone stairs to the Deyang Shar, the easternmost and largest courtyard within the huge Potala. (I later measured this courtyard at 1,900 square yards.) The main building of the Potala rose six stories above the courtyard. This was where the highest officers sat stratified by rank, with the highest floor, of course, belonging to the Dalai Lama.

As the cabinet ministers drank their morning tea on the fourth floor, spectators from Lhasa gathered on the roofs of the lower buildings. The lower officers meanwhile shivered as they, too, sat on rooftops. It was very cold in the morning and they had to arrive early before the ministers got there. They also were grouped by their rank in the feudal nobility.

During the New Year's Eve festival, the Dalai Lama sat on the sixth, or uppermost floor of the center building of the Potala [far left], the Regent on the fifth, the Cabinet Ministers on the fourth, and the Dalai Lama's family on the third. Lower ranking officers [left] wore white hats made of papier mâché as they watched ceremonies in the Deyang Shar courtyard [above].

*Magicians and lamas forced evil spirits into a* torma *made of wood and covered with butter ornaments [above]. The* torma *was later burned to purge the evil spirits from the old year. Earlier, a dancer [left] wearing an apron of human bones performed in the courtyard.*

At the beginning of the ceremony, His Holiness sat behind a curtain on the highest story. But he told me he didn't like to stay there for very long, as it was rather cold and he had to sit quietly because everyone knew he was there. Soon after the ceremony began he would move to the corner room where no one thought he would be and he could watch candidly with his binoculars.

The band, seated under a large canopy, made a great noise with all its drums, cymbals, oboes, and telescopic trumpets. Two trumpets, made of pure silver with gold plating, boomed with such deep resonance that the whole area vibrated. Later, soldiers made even more noise as they fired their old muzzleloading guns, creating a great cloud of smoke. In between, other performers came into the big courtyard. Everybody admired the famous black-hat dancers, whose ritual religious dancing was so strenuous that they had to practice for months before the ceremony.

But the real commotion came if one of spring's first big sandstorms arrived during the ceremony. Everyone would duck and put their long sleeves over their heads, struggling to hold onto their fancy hats. It was dangerous, too, because the band played under a big canopy fixed with long ropes to the other side of the court. When the winds came, this tent would flap and threaten to blow away, dragging the ropes with it. Sometimes the ropes did break and the awning crashed down onto the band. People screamed, a tongue of flame leapt from the *torma*, and the soldiers shot their guns—it was like a drama staged for a great opera. Finally, the old year was driven out.

Then came the reward. Everyone went home and ate *guthug*, the so-called "soup of nine ingredients," which was a great entertainment. The first time I had the pleasure of eating *guthug* was soon after our arrival in Lhasa, at the house of the famous minister, Tsarong. It became a tradition for Aufschnaiter and me to eat this meal with him each year, even after we had our own house. The soup didn't have exactly nine ingredients (the name stems more from the date—the twenty-ninth). It consisted of a few vegetables and a little meat, but the main

*The famous black-hat dancers perform here in the giant Deyang Shar courtyard, which I measured at 1,900 square yards. Lay officers in the government are sitting on the rooftop behind the dancers.*

Monks heat oil [above]
as part of the ceremony
in which the torma will
be burned with a great
flame. In another
ceremony, black-hat
dancers descend the stairs
from the center building
of the Potala [right]
while commoners watch
from a rooftop.

thing is that there were wheat-flour dumplings. Inside one of these dumplings was a lump of charcoal. Everyone would point to and laugh at the person who got the charcoal—he was supposed to have a black, or bad, mind. Then there was one dumpling with a hot pepper in it: that meant the recipient had a sharp tongue. In the next one you might find cotton or wool threads, and that meant you were a good, hard-working person. You could also get a little broken piece of porcelain; this was good, but it made the Tibetans laugh because it meant you liked to eat but not to work. There were many more things you could find in your soup,

including a figure of a man carrying a child on his back. This was bad luck, they said, because children always bring trouble. In the end they pulled out the last big dough figure, which was of a witch. Everything that was in the soup was collected, carried outside on embers, and thrown out with a great shout, thus driving away the old year.

So the day, which had begun so early, ended with great fun and joy, especially for the children. They loved all this shouting and they yelled at the witch to go away. For the grown-ups, it meant that the year ended by destroying all the problems that had plagued their families.

## Monk-Police

A few days after the New Year's celebrations came the Mönlam Chenpo, the Great Prayer. At least 20,000 monks arrived in Lhasa for this event. They were led by the Drepung Monastery's head proctors, called *shälngo*s, who rode into Lhasa on horseback in a big show designed to impress the populace. During the twenty-one days of ceremonies, the city magistrate and all the lay officers withdrew while the *shälngo*s and their monk-police ruled over Lhasa, controlling all Great Prayer–related events. During their time in power, the *shälngo*s kept their own rooms in the Jokhang. They were so dominant that not even the cabinet ministers were allowed to ride horses in Lhasa.

The monks kept the town very, very clean during those weeks. Muscular, black-painted monk-police punished any litterers. But you rarely saw anyone being punished, and the day before the monks arrived women swept the town with willow-twig brooms. Lhasa's populace was very much afraid of the *shälngo*s.

*During the Great Prayer, the monk-police wore thick padding and platform shoes to make themselves look even bigger than they already were, and painted their faces with soot to look fierce. They carried sticks and whips for crowd control.*

The head proctors from
the different faculties at
the Drepung Monastery
ruled over Lhasa during
the Great Prayer. They
carried large iron
scepters to symbolize
their power.

Despite this fear, everyone flocked into the streets for the ceremonies. When the crowds grew too wild, the monk-police threatened them with whips. The people would scream and drop back, then quickly surge forward again.

Each of the faculties from the big monasteries had two head proctors. They were all fierce-looking men. With thickly padded shoulders, platform shoes, and stuffing under their robes, they looked like giants. In their hands they carried a *shag gyu*, a square iron rod that was an emblem of authority. It stood about five feet tall and was covered with gold and silver adornments. When the *shälngo*s demanded attention or silence, they

thumped their rods on the ground. Sometimes they sentenced a rule-breaker to a whipping. But the *shälngo*s would accept money from someone who wanted to avoid being whipped, and I was told that they would go back to Drepung rather rich men.

Whenever the *shälngo*s moved through a crowd, monk-police with big sticks and whips cleared the way for them. With faces blackened with soot, they looked terribly fierce as they shouted, *"Phar-gyu"*: "Make way!" Everybody rushed aside to avoid being whipped. The police didn't just look fierce, many actually were. Some even carried knives in their sleeves. Some of these men were the legendary Dob-Dobs who invited me to do

sports with them at Drepung.

The Dalai Lama's personal bodyguards were not as rough-looking as the monk-police who ruled over Lhasa during Mönlam Chenpo. But they, too, wore heavily-padded clothes that accentuated their already legendary size. These guards averaged over six feet tall. There was even a story of someone who was almost eight feet tall, but he had died young, before I came to Lhasa. During the theater at the summer performances in the garden of Norbulingkha, these guards shouted at the crowd when it got unruly, threatening it with whips. But the whips were more or less symbolic, as they were almost never actually used.

*Monk-police [right]
awed the crowds during
the Great Prayer. As
the State Oracle
approaches [below,
under umbrella], they
clear space for him.
The Dalai Lama's
bodyguards, famed for
their size, watched
over the Norbulingkha
theater [left].*

## King of the Year

At the end of the second Tibetan month, after the Mönlam Chenpo, the "Great Prayer," there was another spectacular festival called Tsongchö Serbang. In this festival two people called *lugong* came, one from the south and one from the north. The one from the south had his face painted half-black and half-white. He was called Lugong Gyälpo, "King of the Year." For the Tibetans he was like a scapegoat.

In front of the Tsuglagkhang the Barkor was crammed with people. Lugong Gyälpo rushed around in the crowd shouting and waving a black yak-tail over their heads, thus transferring all evil to himself. It took no less than Ganden Tri Rinpoche, this learned monk wearing the peaked yellow hat of Tsong Khapa, to finally bring Lugong Gyälpo under control. The crowd would then scream at Lugong Gyälpo to chase him away. This ceremony was highly exciting because everyone was afraid of bad spirits and demons.

Before leaving Lhasa for his homeland of Lhoka, he would go from house to house

Lugong Gyälpo, the
"King of the Year,"
accepts food in the
Nepalese Embassy [left]
after performing in a
ceremony where he
ritualistically drew all
badness to himself. The
policeman with the whip
in his hands [above]
helped to control the
crowd as Lugong
Gyälpo passed by.

collecting money and food. People gave freely because he took evil and ill-luck onto himself for the good of others. When he was satisfied with the gift, he waved a white yak tail. He then went to Samye Monastery on a white horse, where he was supposed to stay one week in the room where souls with bad spirits were tortured by demons. In fact, he didn't really enter this "chamber of horrors" with the demons, instead he would deposit his load of evil in front of the door, then continue his homeward journey.

## *The Day of the* Thangka

Each Tibetan year would begin with the big New Year's Eve ceremony, when the old year was driven out. Then came a break, followed by the Mönlam Chenpo—the Great Prayer—when monks ruled the town, then another break. On the thirtieth day of the second month came a slightly smaller *mönlam*, Tsongchö Tsewang. This was perhaps the most spectacular of all the ceremonies in Tibet, when the largest banners in the world, the giant *thangkas* of present and future Buddhas, were unveiled. Many other ceremonies also took place at the foot of the Potala during the week-long Tsongchö Tsewang that surrounded this event.

Two Masters of Ceremony were responsible for the great *thangka* ceremonies. They were always elite monk officers belonging to the group of Tsedrung, and usually came from aristocratic families. One year my friend Wangdü was appointed to this honored and complicated job; he was responsible for the whole week-long performance. During this week he wore a beautiful monk's cloak that was kept in the treasury of the Tsuglagkhang and belonged to the government.

By far the most important part of this *mönlam* was the difficult and dangerous task of fixing the large *thangkas* below the seven-story-high "Red Palace" section of the Potala. Monks fetched the heavy brocade-and-silk *thangkas* from the Kokukhang, where they were stored during the rest of the year. Ropes were then dropped down to the *thangkas* from the many thick wooden beams that protruded from the interior of the Potala. Each of these beams had a riding saddle lashed onto it, and the most athletic monks sat in these saddles. On orders yelled up from below, the monks would pull up the giant *thangkas* while singing rhythmically. It was a spectacular sight. But since sandstorms could quickly tear the *thangkas* apart, they were only left up for a few hours before the protective silk covering was put back in place and the whole thing was lowered back down again. During a spring storm in 1950, the silk curtain tore. Everyone groaned; this was not a good omen.

*Dancers perform at the foot of the Potala during the great* thangka *ceremony. These two thangkas (portraying present and future Buddhas) were the largest banners in the world.*

157

The many ceremonies surrounding the giant thangkas [left, above] included rügyen dancers from Gongkar [right], wearing aprons of human bones, and the "lazy monks" [left], who got their name because they moved in slow motion during ceremonies.

## Water for the Potala

The Tibetans used water principally to prepare the dozens of bowls of butter tea they drank every day. In the Potala, such needs were not limited to the Dalai Lama and his servants: the 250 learned monks required to attend His Holiness's ceremonies lived up there as well, and another 175 monks of the Tsedrung came up every morning for a meeting where they were served tea and soup. Lhasa had no pipelines to supply water for drinking or other needs. There were a few wells within the city, but during the winter these usually dried up and people had to carry water from the Kyichu River into Lhasa and up to the Potala. Groups of women and children filled wooden or earthenware containers with river water, then carried them about an hour to the Potala and up its many stone stairs. Instead of saving their breath on that steep stairway, they sang as they climbed. Carrying water for use in the Potala was a form of taxation in a society where taxes were paid in labor and goods rather than in money.

The most precious water in Tibet came from a stone-wall–enclosed spring at the foot of Chagpori. This was the Dalai Lama's personal water, and special mules carried it up a road on the north side of the Potala. Excess water often flowed through a hole in the wall. Anyone could use this overflow, as well as the mineral spring in a cave not far away. When it flowed, this holy spring was the principal water source for the monks living in the Potala.

After we had lived in Lhasa for a while, Aufschnaiter and I suggested that we pump water to the top of the Potala. As I planned out how to move the water with a diesel pump, I practiced by making a primitive fountain in Tsarong's garden. I put a tank on top of his house, which was about twenty feet high, and ran a pipe down into the flower garden. I then installed a little fountain in the garden that was activated by water pressure from above. Servants carried buckets of water up to the tank on the roof. This fountain was a great sensation in Lhasa and many children came there to play.

*Women and children carried water up to the many monks living in the Potala. Often they had to bring it from the Kyichu River, an hour's walk away.*

In the morning Lhasa's only elephant [left], the survivor of a pair given by the king of Nepal, drank at the Dalai Lama's personal spring [below]. In big ceremonies, the elephant was adorned with brocade and ornaments. Most monks in the Potala used water from another spring [right] under Chagpori.

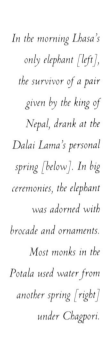

## Arrow Letters and Postal Runners

Though Lhasa had a post office, Tibet did not belong to the world postal union and did not even have regular mail distribution within the country. Friends who happened to travel somewhere carried most private letters inside Tibet. Between Lhasa and Tibet's borders, postal runners ran in relays of about four miles, carrying international mail in a cloth bundle over their shoulders. These runners were drawn from the local population along the caravan routes. As part of their taxation these people had to provide a man every week to carry the mail.

As a sign of his importance, and also to defend himself against occasional attacks by bears, the mail-runner carried a spear with bells on it. The bells also forewarned of his approach to a house or a nomad tent so the next runner could prepare himself.

Important or urgent government messages were written on a red cloth and wrapped around an arrow. These were called *da-yig*— *da* means arrow and *yig* means letter. En-

trusted with one of these letters, a postal runner could get good horses for traveling longer distances at greater speed than were used for a normal letter. Even so, the mail didn't always move fast enough. Once, the government in Lhasa sent one of these arrow letters to a military outpost at Tibet's northern border. The letter, which gave the American consul general in Mongolia permission to take his caravan through the country, arrived a day too late. The Tibetan army had already shot the consul general and one of his attendants when they arrived at the border.

Because Tibet did not belong to the world postal union, its stamps had value only inside Tibet. Typically, letters to foreign countries would have Tibetan stamps on one side and stamps from India on the other—or the envelope with Indian stamps would be put inside an envelope with Tibetan stamps.

For almost three years, my parents didn't know where I was. They had heard from my friends in the internment camp that I had escaped. What happened next, nobody knew. But after we had been several months in

Postal runners traveled
in relay stages of about
four miles each, carrying
letters in a pouch. This
runner is traveling
between Gyangtse and
Shigatse.

*The lay governor of Gyangtse [left] reads a red arrow letter held by one of his secretaries. It carries important government communications. The governor of Tsang [above], whose capital was Shigatse, had one of the most profitable jobs. Here he writes a letter.*

Lhasa the British trade mission permitted Peter Aufschnaiter and me to send letters to Europe once a month via their special service to Europe (using their own postal runners to Gyangtse). Ours was considered POW mail because our camp in India still operated, complete with all my fellow inmates from when I escaped almost three years earlier. To use the British mail, we had to write our letters on a typewriter and they were censored. Later on it became much easier to get mail out, but even when the system worked well, it took three to six months to get a reply.

I later designed a whole series of about forty different stamps in the hope that Tibet would join the world postal union. The stamps bore drawings of famous buildings in Lhasa and surroundings, of Tibet's beautiful flowers, of the eight good-luck signs, and of the most important animals, like sheep, yaks, and goats. But the Chinese arrived before these stamps could come into use.

## The Drepung Monastery

Visiting the monastery called Drepung, about a one-hour ride from Lhasa (roughly five miles), became one of my favorite excursions. Drepung was at the foot of the mountains and had a view of the Kyichu, the holy river that flows past Lhasa. Officially with 7,700 monks (in fact there were many more), Drepung was the largest monastery in the world. Along with Sera and Ganden, slightly smaller monasteries, it was one of "the three pillars of Tibet" and of the Tibetan government. Each of these monasteries was very well organized, with its own government, financial department (because they owned fields), and judiciary. Only the Chikyab Khenpo and the Dalai Lama ranked higher than the abbots of these monasteries, who sat in the National Assembly.

The most esteemed monks were the incarnate lamas addressed as *rinpoche*s, meaning "precious ones." They were considered living gods who had already reached nirvana but had returned to earth to save more souls. One of the highest *rinpoche*s in Drepung was a good friend of mine, Thubten Jigme Norbu, the eldest brother of the Dalai Lama. His room was a bit larger than those of the ordinary monks and he had a small kitchen where he or his cook would prepare our most beloved food, the famous Tibetan *momo*. These are a kind of steamed dumpling that Norbu made especially beautifully, singing while he worked. Occasionally his younger brother Lobsang Samten came to Drepung, as did other friends. We spent wonderful times together in this monastery.

Of course a *rinpoche* has responsibilities, and while Norbu conducted his prayers, I went around in the monastery. It was like a large city, with parks and big trees to shade the monks engaged in their daily debates on logic. Not more than ten percent of the monks were really educated; the common, uneducated monks had enough to do around the monastery. One of their most difficult jobs was tending the enormous kitchens with their giant cauldrons. When I went into Drepung's main kitchen, I could hardly see

*The monks at Drepung loved pomp as much as anyone else, and they especially enjoyed the annual ceremony during which they unrolled their giant* thangka.

Large trees shade student monks debating questions of logic with their teachers [left]. The abbots of the monastery control the great thangka ceremony. Here they sit on cushions, small tables holding their cups of butter tea [right]. Spectators cover the hillside [below], many picnicking as they enjoy the festival.

the workers because the place was so full of smoke and steam. There were no windows, just a hole in the ceiling. It was a fantastic image to see a ray of sun angling from this hole down through the smoke.

Once a year there was a great festival at Drepung that I was certain to visit. Many people from Lhasa and pilgrims from everywhere in Tibet came to attend this big ceremony, called Shutun. The Tibetans love pomp and processions, and took every opportunity to look at the beautiful clothes and ornaments worn by the aristocracy; even the higher clerical officers wore expensive brocade.

The Shutun Festival celebrated the annual change of administration at Drepung. The main ceremonial event was unrolling a giant *thangka* on the hillside. This *thangka* was perhaps second only to the one unfurled on the Potala after the New Year. The Drepung monks were always joyful during this ceremony. They, too, loved pomp—but they also knew they would soon get presents, perhaps even money from wealthy onlookers. The abbots who directed the day's events sat below the great *thangka* while spectators sat scattered along the slope, picnicking and enjoying the grand spectacle.

## The Rain Oracle

Gadong, the well-known rain oracle, lived about one-and-a-half hours riding distance from Lhasa. The monastery of Drepung had a close connection with Gadong because it owned a lot of fields in his region. One year there was an extended drought, and several monks and I rode to visit Gadong for his advice.

Gadong belonged to a famous group of oracles called *chokyong*, "defenders of the faith." His reputation came from being able to conjure up the water spirits. In private with my best Tibetan friends I sometimes mentioned that I had doubts about the Gadong's abilities. They patiently explained that the rain oracle's mother was *klu*, meaning she was half-human and half-snake and was the goddess of water. Therefore when he fell into trance he could speak with the spirit of the goddess of water. Gadong could marry and his ability was evidently hereditary.

When we met with him during the drought, the Drepung monks asked for rain on their fields. As offerings, they brought him a sheep carcass and a pouch full of silver coins. With incense clouding the room, Gadong slipped into trance. After some time, he blew into a human thigh-bone trumpet and rapidly turned his child-skull *damaru* drum to summon the spirits. Attendants rushed around during the complicated ceremonies, finally putting a massive cone-shaped ornament onto his head. He slumped under the weight as they strapped it under his chin, then began to slowly rotate on one foot, the other leg slightly lifted. A mystic hush pervaded the room, mantras were said, and the deep chanting voices of the monks filled the air along with the sounds of cymbals and drums. While Gadong slowly turned in his heavy outfit, the petitioner neared him with a *khatag* extended and asked for rain. Gadong threw rice toward the petitioner and mumbled something his interpreter-assistants wrote down. When Gadong swung his sword I moved back, not sure whether he had control in his trance. I was filled with awe at the proceedings. Then he collapsed.

*The rain oracle's head ornament was so heavy it took two assistants to place it on his head. After rotating on one foot while in a trance, he eventually collapsed. Oracles never lived very long.*

In our case, the interpreters told us that to bring rain we were to go up the mountain Gephe Utse, make offerings, and follow the rules of Migtsemai Letsog, the rain-compelling sorcery. The scripture promised that rain was coming.

In Lhasa there was also an amusing custom for bringing on the rain after a long drought. Suddenly, without warning, the populace erupted in a water festival. Walking through the Barkor, I was drenched when a surprise bucket of water was thrown at me. Everyone there got soaked, no one escaped. The streets rang with laughter and everyone called *"gongda, gongda"* meaning "excuse me, excuse me." The Tibetans had no idea of physics—that evaporating water made clouds and clouds made rain—but this ceremony surely worked, because eventually the thunder dragon came and it always rained again.

## The Wool and Salt Trade

I don't know how many millions of sheep there were in Tibet, but their wool was Tibet's biggest export and provided the greatest income for the nomads. The meat, always air dried, we could buy in Lhasa. But wool earned the big profits. One load, called a "mound" in India, was about ninety pounds. Poorer nomads carried these loads themselves to the Indian border town of Kalimpong, where there were large trading posts owned by rich Tibetans.

In Kalimpong the traders told me they had to be very careful because of cheating. The richest Tibetan trader was a man named Pangdatshang Rimshi. He told me that he could buy wool without concern from the simple nomads, because they never cheated. But he was always very careful dealing with large caravans carrying thousands of bales. Each bale had to weigh ninety pounds, but sometimes wet sand was injected into the

*Each yak in a caravan carried two ninety-pound "mounds" of wool on its back. The caravan often took weeks or even months to cross the Changthang.*

bales. The traders in Kalimpong used long thin iron hooks to pull out samples from the interior of the bale to check its quality.

Yaks would carry two of these bales, 180 pounds, across the high plateau of Changthang. But since they could not survive below 10,000 feet, when they reached the Yatung Valley near the Indian border, the yaks went back and the wool was transferred onto mules, horses, or porters for the carry to Kalimpong.

Kalimpong was near Darjeeling, the 6,500-foot-high mountain village. Here lived some of the wealthiest Tibetan traders; they had big houses and could handle up to 200 mules

*After shearing the sheep [above], poor Tibetans sometimes carried the ninety-pound bales [right] to such distant markets as Kalimpong on their own backs.*

Since yaks cannot
survive below 10,000
feet, the wool
transported by yak
caravan had to be
transferred to mules
and other carriers
before reaching India.

loaded with wool. They stored the wool here until buyers came from foreign countries. Sadutshang, another wealthy trader from the nobility, told me the best buyers came from the United States because the Americans had found out that this wool, which was not very good for making soft clothes or sweaters, was the best for carpets.

When Aufschnaiter and I lived in Kyirong during our escape to Lhasa, we saw 5,000 or 10,000 sheep from the highlands of Tibet being brought through the narrow and steep gorges between Dzonga and the Nepalese border, eight miles south of Kyirong. It was a big show because most of these sheep were carrying about fifteen to twenty pounds of salt on their backs, and there was only one steep, narrow path. The sheep would scatter everywhere along the slopes, sometimes climbing down cliffs. Often the animals slipped, occasionally falling to their deaths in the gorge. It took them hours to pass our place.

Most of the sheep carried two little sacks of salt. Salt was free for the collecting in the highlands of Tibet. There were big lakes with no outlets—water came in and evaporated, leaving large plains of salt. Nomads put it in little bags made of yak or sheep wool, sewed up the openings, and then the sheep carried it down to Nepal. Often the nomads took their sheep further south to India, which was twice the distance. Then they could sell both the sheep and the salt.

Halfway to India, somewhere south of the main chain of the Himalayas, was a place where the exchange of salt to barley or rice was one to one—one "*bo*" of salt for one "*bo*" of rice or barley. But when you carried your wool or salt, whatever you were trading, farther south, then you had a different exchange rate: You got more rice for less salt. And the other way around: If you exchanged it before the halfway place, you got less for the salt and paid more for the rice or barley.

## Yaks

The yak is the most important animal in Tibet. Technically, the word "yak" refers only to the castrated bull. Westerners often refer to yak butter, as in "yak butter tea." This brings a smile to the Tibetans—it is as if we were to speak of oxen or bull butter. The female is called *dri*, while the bull has a name that varies from region to region. Nevertheless, the term yak has become synonymous with all Tibetan cattle.

Yaks live only in the highlands. The animal can live down to about 11,000 feet, but if you bring it much lower it soon dies. I discovered this when we were on our escape to Lhasa. We had bought a wonderful yak for not much money. It had no horns and wore a juniper ring through the septum in its nose. I would lead the yak with a goat-hair rope from the front while Aufschnaiter walked behind. We crossed many high passes this way, while the yak carried 100 to 150 pounds of our belongings.

When the Tibetans ordered us to go to Nepal, we took the yak with us. People warned us against this, saying, "If you go down that low, your yak will die." We didn't really believe this, thinking they just wanted to buy the yak from us cheaply. But they were right. After a week in Kyirong, which was only 10,000 feet high, the yak got ill. We tried everything to save it, we even visited a famous Tibetan doctor who sold me an expensive gallbladder of a bear. But despite this medicine our yak got worse. Finally we had to have it slaughtered by a Nepalese blacksmith. At least we could use some of its meat. It turns out you can bring a yak down to 8,000 feet to drop off a load, but it needs to return to its high pastures that day. At the altitude where they live, yaks have lots of energy. I have even seen yak races; these were wild, wild performances with riders galloping along on these giant animals.

Yak caravans couldn't travel very far in a day because the yaks had to feed themselves along the way. Yaks have very long tongues, and while walking they lick seeds from the ground or get the long dry grass growing in

*Nyima, my personal servant, rides a yak led by its owner during one of our excursions into the mountains. Here we're crossing the pass called Drip La, on the way to Samye.*

the Changthang. So a caravan would travel only four to six hours, and the rest of the day the yaks would be let loose for grazing. In the evening they were collected and kept in a group to be guarded from wolves and leopards.

The long underfur from the yak is very fine and warm, and the Tibetans make clothes out of it, while coarse outer hair is used for making yak-hair tents. The most interesting export from the yak was its tail. This hair is long and shiny and comes in many colors:

brown, black, white, and mixed. Black tails are the most common; and pure white ones are the most expensive. Several hundred bales of yak tails were exported every year, used for tassels and for special ornaments for helmets and uniforms, including those of the king of Nepal and the maharajahs in India. The tails are also used as dusters and, until nylon was invented, yak tails were considered to make the most beautiful beards for St. Nicholas in European Christmas ceremonies.

A yak caravan [left]
loads next to the south
wall of Shö in front of
the Potala. On route
yaks graze during every
rest stop since they are
never provided with
fodder. The yaks
with riding saddles
[right] are on their
way to Samye.

## Norbulingkha Procession

The Dalai Lama had two residences, the Potala for the winter season and the Norbulingkha, that beautiful "jewel garden," for the summer. After a cold winter spent nearly alone inside the highest story of the Potala, the young Fourteenth Dalai Lama was always delighted when the time came to move down to the verdant Norbulingkha.

A huge procession accompanied the Dalai Lama when he moved from one residence to the other and thousands of people lined the road, all in awe of His Holiness. Everyone would bow down as he passed, no one daring to look up. His appearance so close to them was considered a blessing.

Twelve men wearing broad-brimmed red hats carried the Dalai Lama in a sedan chair. Twenty more men held ropes attached to the palanquin, symbolically helping to carry His Holiness. His horses also came along for symbolic reasons, while all of his baggage followed on a long train of mules. The whole procession moved down a road built at an

*Every spring, the Dalai Lama moved from the Potala [right] to his "jewel garden," the Norbulingkha. In a journey full of symbolism, an important abbot [above] precedes one of His Holiness's horses.*

*The Dalai Lama rode to and from the Norbulingkha in a big palanquin [far left]. His belongings [left] followed behind his chamberlain, a very important monk. The Dalai Lama delighted at the beauty of Norbulingkha, including the temple in the lake [above].*

*In the autumn
procession returning to
the Potala [above] the
first two umbrellas
belong to His Holiness,
the third to the Regent.
The banners [left,
above] go on top of
important temples like
the Potala. The three-
pointed symbol
represents flames. Each
garpa drummer [left]
has one deep-sounding
drum representing the
male voice and one
with a higher pitch
representing the female.*

elevation to keep the Dalai Lama above the swamp. This was the only raised road constructed in Lhasa.

In front of the Dalai Lama was a bright-green umbrella of peacock feathers, while behind him followed an umbrella made of brocade. Because the Fourteenth Dalai Lama was only a minor, the Regent rode behind him under an umbrella to show his own importance. The whole procession was full of such symbolism. There was even a white horse to represent the Mongols when they had control over Tibet during the fourteenth century. Drummers on horseback rode by with their special drums symbolic of male and female voices. Much of the nobility participated, all dressed up in their finest garments. The procession to and from the Norbulingkha was always a spectacular sight, never to be missed.

## The Ferry

While pedestrians often floated down the Tsangpo River on yak-skin boats, horse caravans had to cross on wooden ferries in order to continue down the other bank. Sometimes the heavy ferries used ropes to keep from being swept downstream in the fast current, but often they relied exclusively on the hard work of the oarsmen and women.

One of the main crossing points was known as the Chagsam ("iron bridge") Ferry. This crossing got its name because there was once a chain-link bridge there, one of many built by the revered Thangdong Gyalpo in the fifteenth century. This place was important in recent history as well, as this was where the legendary Tsarong Sawang Chenpo (father of George Tsarong) earned his position as the "favorite" of the Thirteenth Dalai Lama. As a young man he had defended this crossing against the pursuing Chinese in 1910, providing the Dalai Lama with enough time to make his getaway.

*Ropes often helped keep the wooden ferries from drifting downstream at the Chagsam crossing, where women, like this nun [left], pulled on the oars along with the men.*

It was a lot of work to take a big caravan across the Tsangpo River. Prayer flags above a carved wooden horse's head [far right, bow of boat] helped provide the necessary good luck.

## Master Craftsmen

Often in Lhasa you would meet someone from whose left ear dangled a long and beautiful golden earring, inset with turquoise and genuine pearls. This meant he was a master of his craft, a so-called *um-dze*. *Um-dze*s included masons, writers, and many others and were represented by guilds in the 400-member general assembly of deputies. The long earring that identified them, which was also worn by noblemen, was called a *so-ji*. Lower-ranking professionals, like boatmen, could wear a round earring called *a-long* when they achieved status.

On especially important projects, the government always employed these *um-dze*. One such project was building a new *chörten* next to the Western Gate, or Bagogaling. When the Chinese threat began, the whole city grew fearful. Hoping faith would protect Tibet, the government ordered more prayer flags to be fixed in the mountains, new prayer wheels to be made, and the construction of this new *chörten*. Holy scripts, relics, and offerings made of clay went inside the *chörten*.

*With his* so-ji *earring dangling, this master craftsman builds a new* chörten *next to the Western Gate. Pincers in hand, an* um-dze *[right] blows through a pipe into hot coals as he makes a tiny golden amulet.*

## Expulsion of the Chinese

Whenever the Chinese had internal difficulties, the Tibetans would make a big point of declaring their neutrality. The Chinese delegation in Lhasa was staffed by Nationalists, and, as the Communist revolution progressed, the Tibetans finally asked the delegation to leave Lhasa and Tibet.

In July 1949, the Tibetan government held a feast for the Chinese and presented them with *khatags*, the white good-luck scarves. Then, to the sound of a Tibetan band, and with Tibetan soldiers saluting, the Chinese delegation left Lhasa on horseback. It was typical for the Tibetans to be so polite. A delegation of Tibetan soldiers accompanied them as far as the border with Sikkim. The Chinese obviously couldn't be sent back home, because the communists were there.

In the pictures we can see that hardly anyone took notice that the Chinese were departing. But actually many of us were sorry

The Chinese
Ambassador [left, far
left side of picture]
leaves his quarters in
Lhasa. His servants
[above] ride through the
famous Yuthoksampa,
the turquoise-colored
bridge.

*With his white good-*
*luck scarf tucked under*
*his raincoat, the Chinese*
*Ambassador [below, in*
*the foreground] rides*
*out of Lhasa during*
*his expulsion. The*
*Chinese entourage*
*soon filed through the*
*swampy land outside*
*Lhasa [right].*

they had to leave Lhasa. I had very close contact with the Chinese. The first secretary, Shen Chi Liu, was one of the friends with whom I played tennis every week at the British Mission, and at least twice a year we met during special Chinese holidays in the embassy itself. They had an excellent cook, and I, along with other foreigners, was very merry there. Even British representative Hugh Richardson, otherwise rather reserved, usually ended up not sitting at the table, but lying on the carpet with everyone else, arguing. Despite our political differences, we were all good friends.

## The Dalai Lama's Escape

When it seemed the Communist Chinese were about to reach Lhasa, the Dalai Lama made his escape. I accompanied him during most of his journey to the Chumbi Valley, on the Tibetan side of the border with India. After two weeks of travel, we crossed the 17,000-foot Karola Pass and dropped to the twenty-mile-long plain of Tuna.

It was bitterly cold on this plain, and the wind nearly knocked us off our feet. In fact the cold was so intense that His Holiness sat in his sedan chair only when he was passing settlements and protocol dictated he must be inside. Whenever he could, he walked to keep from freezing.

Tibetans had put up prayer flags all along the Dalai Lama's escape route, and they burned incense for him at every possible occasion. For nearly the whole distance— maybe 300 miles—they had placed white stones to prevent evil spirits from crossing his path. Whenever we passed a settlement or a monastery, everyone would come out to pros-trate and to offer *khatag*s to His Holiness, who sat freezing in his cold sedan chair. Only after he had long passed the settlement could he get out to walk so his blood could circulate again.

We finally reached Phari and soon were descending from the high plains on the roof of the world through deep gorges to the forested Chumbi Valley and the village of Yatung. As His Holiness was carried through Yatung, the whole population came to see. The night air was filled with incense and the snow came lightly down. Soon we reached the monastery of Dungkhar, where we stayed for the next three months.

People from the entire region came to get blessings from His Holiness. After he was here some weeks, an Indian Buddhist society came up to visit. They brought the young Dalai Lama a precious relic: a golden urn that contained a 2,500-year-old bone fragment from Gautama Buddha himself. I photo-graphed this beautiful ceremony, and these became the last pictures of the Dalai Lama in free Tibet.

The entire local populace would always turn out for the Dalai Lama's passage. Here he arrives in his sedan chair at the monastery of Gyangtse. The white stones were placed along the Dalai Lama's route to keep evil spirits from crossing his path.

Incense burned in honor of the Dalai Lama [right] whenever he passed a settlement. The governor of Phari [left, right side of photo] and assistants greet the Dalai Lama after he crossed the plains, where he had to walk to keep from freezing [above, second from left]. Surkhang Wangchuk [right, above] uses a field telephone during the flight.

*The Dalai Lama receiving a precious
relic of Gautama Buddha in a special ceremony
at Dungkhar Monastery near the Indian border.*

# ESCAPE TO INDIA

During the summer of 1950 I grew increasingly concerned about the threat from Communist China, and I repeatedly told the Tibetan authorities that I thought the Communists would be even more intolerant than the Chinese invaders who had sporadically occupied the country in the past, earlier in the century. In October, after listening to the news on a battery-operated radio, I brought His Holiness the information that the Chinese were approaching; in fact, they already occupied parts of eastern Tibet. It was obvious to me that they would pounce on the remainder of Tibet sometime soon, most likely when the rivers were low. The Tibetan army was ill-equipped and weak; they couldn't be expected to stop the invaders. And Tibet could count on no aid from the outside. The people of Lhasa became resigned to their fate.

His Holiness thought Peter Aufschnaiter and I should leave Lhasa, and I talked this over with my old friend. He had been a soldier in World War I—in the Dolomites—and then he spent World War II in camps in India with me. Now, as a third war threatened—this time in Tibet, where he would have least expected it—he simply wished to stay put.

But I decided to heed the advice of the Dalai Lama, who told me: "Go now, Henrig [Henrig is what the Tibetans called me]; you have worked hard. We will meet again." He was right; we would meet again, much sooner than we thought. It was absurd that I had to leave this most peaceful country. Who would have thought that it would be Tibet, of all places in the world, that I would be driven away from by war? In early November I left Lhasa with a group of important Tibetans. Saying farewell to the Holy City, we embarked yak-hide coracles and floated down the Kyichu River toward its junction with the Tsangpo, six hours downstream. I could not keep my eyes off the Potala as we drifted along, knowing that the Dalai Lama was watching our departure through his binoculars.

A week later I reached the town of Gyangtse on the great caravan route connecting Tibet with India. A good friend of mine had recently been appointed governor of this region and I stayed in his house. In a few days messengers arrived bearing a scroll letter on a red cloth saying that the Fourteenth Dalai Lama had ascended to the throne—one year early because of the upcoming troubles. Local Tibetans rejoiced at this news and began dancing; the *chang* flowed and everyone was elated.

I was in no great hurry to leave Tibet, so I journeyed fifty miles west to Shigatse, the country's second-largest city. This reminded me of Lhasa, since it was also dominated by a fortress. I met a number of my friends in Shigatse, and they were all eager to hear the news from the capital.

Not long after my return to Gyangtse, we heard that His Holiness had left Lhasa under the cover of night and was approaching; he had decided to flee Lhasa. My friend the governor became very busy since he was responsible for the transport of the Dalai Lama through his region. The rough parts of the roads were repaired, and the people put white lines and rows of stones on both sides of the escape route in order to prevent evil spirits from crossing the path.

The governor was also responsible for obtaining fodder for the animals, and with finding peas and barley for the Dalai Lama's entourage. The town and its people were busy indeed. With a number of servants, a small group of us rode our horses in the direction of Lhasa for three days in order to meet His Holiness at Karo Pass, the high pass between Lhasa and Gyangtse. From here we saw in the distance a cloud of dust: the Dalai Lama's column approached. His Holiness was carried in a little sedan chair and in his entourage were about several hundred soldiers and forty noblemen, all on horseback. The caravan contained more than a thousand animals. It was an impressive sight.

Among the caravan was one of His Holiness's older brothers, my good friend Lobsang. He had suffered a heart attack during the journey and had been treated by a Tibetan doctor who had put a branding iron to his flesh, which brought him back to consciousness. He told me this story and many others about their departure. They had left Lhasa at two in the morning after having a tea-drinking ceremony to ensure their speedy return. None of the rooms in the Potala were cleaned that next day, for to do so would bring bad luck to His Holiness.

Although the Dalai Lama's flight was supposed to be secret, thousands of people lined the route outside Lhasa; monks and even nuns flung themselves in front of the

*The Surkhang family [top] and me next to a Tibetan-style dike at the riverside just before fleeing Lhasa. Two flags flew during the Dalai Lama's escape, his personal flag and the Tibetan national flag; the latter featured two snow lions in a white mountain holding up a norbu, the precious Tibetan gem.*

horses and begged His Holiness not to leave, feeling they would be at the mercy of the Chinese. The Dalai Lama convinced them he could do more for his country if he was safe outside Tibet. He promised to return as soon as possible.

We left southward from Gyangtse not long afterward, and after sixteen days arrived at our provisional destination, Chumbi, only a few miles short of the border with Sikkim.

From here I made excursions every day, sometimes with Lobsang, who was recovering nicely, and also with Norbu. Once we went up to Sikkim's border, and I realized I simply didn't want to leave. But one day I heard that the government-in-exile, after dealing with the Chinese and getting the Seventeen-Point Agreement, intended to go back to Lhasa. I told them that I would not return because I was afraid of staying under Communist rule. I requested the government grant me official leave so that I could return when the time came.

*I spent several months in the Chumbi Valley, which felt like a green oasis after those years in the arid interior of Tibet. With sadness in my heart, I finally decided to leave Tibet rather than return to a Lhasa ruled by the Communists.*

I was still trying to hang on, and occasionally Lobsang and I went out with His Holiness to visit the local monasteries of the Chumbi Valley. These excursions marked the first time that His Holiness had ever had the opportunity to take physical exercise outside his palaces. He was so energetic we could hardly keep up with him.

Indian monks arrived one day with a golden urn containing a precious relic of the Lord Buddha. On this occasion I took my final and best photo of the Fourteenth Dalai Lama; it was the very last photo made of His Holiness in free Tibet. I felt a deep anxiety about the young god-king, knowing that his country would soon be under the iron thumb of Mao Tse-tung.

In March 1951, I realized that my time in Tibet was over, so I left Chumbi and crossed into Sikkim, and then into India. On one of the frontier passes, brightly colored prayer flags fluttered in the breeze. In Lhasa, though, the red-colored hammer and sickle of the Chinese Communists flew over the city.

It had been nearly seven years since my companions and I had first entered Tibet. I took my horse's reins in my hand and walked slowly down toward the plains of India.

A few days later I was in Kalimpong, once again among Europeans. They looked odd to me, and I felt like a stranger in their presence. It took me a long time to acclimatize myself to the hustle of civilization. Meanwhile, the Dalai Lama returned to Lhasa to find posters of Mao plastered against the walls of the Potala.

When I returned in 1982, I found that the Chinese
had destroyed the medical school that perched
atop Chagpori and replaced it with a radio tower.

# EPILOGUE

More than forty years have passed since I returned from Asia, and, though I have made numerous expeditions to other interesting places, the seven years I spent in Tibet remain my happiest.

When I broke out of the internment camp in the spring of 1944, it was called a successful escape. But I think this is the wrong expression for what I had done. I didn't have to escape *from* anything: I didn't suffer hardship, repression, or hunger. It was actually the opposite: my stay in the camp was pleasant. I had books, sporting activities, and good rations. The British treated us according to the Geneva Convention.

It was I who wanted to get away, it was I who wanted to reach something. Maybe my dash toward freedom was sport; maybe it was done to outsmart the guards; maybe it was simply a continuation of what I had been doing earlier in my life: facing up to a challenge.

Quite different was my reason for leaving Tibet seven years later. Peter Aufschnaiter and I had become Tibetans; we wanted to stay there the rest of our lives. Despite demands from the outside world, we never sold pictures or articles while we were living there. We corresponded only with our relatives and with the legendary Sven Hedin in Stockholm, who had explored Tibet years earlier.

I tried for thirty years to reenter Tibet and was rebuffed each time. Finally, in 1982, I joined a group of sixty tourists, mostly Americans, and was able to get into Lhasa before the Chinese realized who I was. From earlier reports, I thought I knew what I was going to see, but the reality was far worse than I expected.

Except for the Potala, which had become a museum with an entrance fee, practically everything had been destroyed. Thanks to the Chinese, all but a handful of Tibet's six thousand buildings, shrines, and monasteries had been eradicated. And more than a million Tibetans, one-fifth of the population, had lost their lives during the upheavals.

Some of the old women in the bazaar recognized me with tears in their eyes, but the younger ones were flabbergasted when they heard me speaking the Lhasa dialect. Soon

I was surrounded by people asking for pictures of His Holiness. I quietly distributed many such illegal photographs, and it was heartwarming to see the people immediately touching the pictures to their foreheads. Then they would quickly hide them under their shirts. (A year later a tourist was fined $1,000 for possessing pictures of His Holiness. And I later read in *Time* magazine that another tourist was forced to leave Lhasa because he had my book. It amuses me to think that my little book gives headaches to a large nation like China.)

When I saw my old friends in Lhasa, the word they used most was *dzüma*, which means "sham" or "hogwash." By this they meant things weren't as they appeared on the surface, that the Chinese were always trying to hide what Tibetans really felt. There was, at all times, a subtle rebellion going on. I was told that unmarried Lhasa girls sing a song about choosing a husband, saying they would prefer a Tibetan with a smallpox-scarred face to a Chinese. As soon as the Chinese knew who I was (which wasn't hard once we reached Lhasa), they assigned a special Chinese guide to accompany me at all times.

I went to see all those places I had worked with Peter Aufschnaiter. The houses I had lived in were now occupied by Chinese officers. One house where I had established a beautiful flower garden had been burned down by Tibetan rebels because it had stored Chinese documents incriminating residents of Lhasa. I felt proud when I saw the dike

*The view from the Potala once extended over vast gardens. Now the landscape is covered by steel shacks.*

along the Kyichu River that Peter Aufschnaiter and I had built: it was still functional. Some of the canals we had built still existed also.

Lhasa was as dirty as ever, even though we had made a fine map of the city to aid in building a sewer system. The Chinese, after decades of occupation, had apparently made few improvements. And I was shocked to see that they had destroyed the famous Western Gate, through which we had arrived with pounding hearts after our long, long journey. A wide road sliced through this area now, and military convoys and large rocket-carrying vehicles moved through.

Even worse, to my eyes, was the disappearance of the medical school atop Chagpori, the second-highest hill of Lhasa. The hill now sported a television mast. The Tsuglagkhang, a large temple with golden roofs in the center of the town, had been built in the seventh century and luckily still stood intact. But the atmosphere of the place was destroyed because the large willows that had stood in front of the entrance had disappeared. During the Cultural Revolution, Tsuglagkhang had served as a hotel for Chinese officers. Then it became a cinema. Only after tourists came to Tibet was the temple restored. The famous bell was missing; years later remnants were found in an attic along with other bronze fragments.

At first I couldn't find the beautiful Turquoise Bridge, but then I discovered it crammed in between new houses. There was no access to the inside of the bridge, but I could see it was full of old carriages and so on. I looked in vain for the slender stone obelisk at the foot of the Potala; it took me some time to learn that it had been removed to a spot farther east. In the old days pilgrims would tap it with small stones in order to take back a few grains of sand, which they considered medicine. Now the Chinese had pretended to protect the magnificent obelisk by putting a wall around it. I also imagine the Chinese didn't want the people to see the ancient inscriptions that said the Chinese had to pay 50,000 rolls of silk and brocade annually to the Tibetan government.

Soon after my arrival in Lhasa a handsome man in a black leather jacket approached me and said, "Don't you recognize me, Henrig?" I was puzzled; after all, it had been thirty years! "You saved my life," he said. Then I remembered. During a party given by the Tibetan foreign minister on the banks of the Kyichu, a young boy had been carried away by the current. I had jumped in, pulled him ashore, and given him artificial respiration. (Tragically, in 1990 he was killed when he crashed his motorbike into a truck in Lhasa.)

With my guide along, there were few opportunities to talk to old friends and listen to their stories. But I managed to hear a few tales. Some told of death by torture and starvation. And I learned some old friends of mine had committed suicide. The most tragic of these involved my dear friend Tsarong, that wonderful, hospitable man in whose house I had lived for so long. He had fled to India but longed for home; he believed that since he got along with all the other foreigners, he would also get along with the Chinese. But when he returned to Lhasa, he was jailed. One day, when it was clear that he was going to be tried in the People's Court, he took an action he had once described to me. He had said that if he ever got into problems and was taken prisoner, he would swallow the contents of a little bag of diamond splinters that he carried with him always. That is apparently what he did.

Another one of my friends also committed suicide. Tsecha-Gyeltsen and his friend Shöl-tsedön went to Norbulingkha and ascended the little platform where the Tibetan theater performed. They stood facing each other, counted to three, then shot one another.

The Potala and the Tsuglagkhang were both damaged by gunfire, but they were entirely repaired and nothing can be seen of the damage. When I went to Sera Monastery, I saw that the building had been repaired in front, where the tourists come. But in the rear the buildings had been destroyed. In the distance I could also see the place where the Tibetans cut up their corpses, and I was upset to find that the site had become a tourist attraction.

The third-largest monastery, Ganden, was so devastated that it was beyond repair. I also went to the largest monastery, Drepung, to the west, but no one lived there either.

I made a side trip south from the capital to visit Gyangtse, the first city I stayed in after fleeing Lhasa in 1951. I had fond memories of the place, but now factories rose everywhere.

I also visited Norbulingkha, the summer palace of the Dalai Lama. This had been damaged but was now repaired. After His Holiness's return in 1951, the Tibetans built a little house for him which contained beautiful frescoes, one of which portrayed practically all the officers who were in power during my time. I stood for a long time gazing at the faces of individuals I had known so well.

I badly wanted to see Wangdü, my best friend during my time in Lhasa. This proved difficult. When I arrived at the airport I had been met by a pretty Tibetan woman named Drölma, one of the daughters of Tsarong. She was now married to Wangdü, so I asked her if I could see her husband. She agreed. But whenever I tried to arrange a meeting, it seemed impossible. One day a Chinese officer told me I must apply in writing. More time passed. On my very last evening I reminded this officer of his promise to get me an audience with Wangdü, and he finally relented.

The officer gave me a Russian jeep and a driver, and my guide and I went off to see him at his residence east of Lhasa. I knew that Wangdü had become a collaborator. But when I met him, in the darkness of the evening, it was evident that both of us were moved. He put his arm around my shoulder and led me into one of his rooms. He radiated a lot of charm; I remembered the old days when a number of pretty Lhasa girls had fallen for him.

Wangdü lit one cigarette after the other as his eleven-year-old son refilled our teacups. He told me that he was in charge of the Potala and also of tourist excursions. I asked him whether we later could go down to the Brahmaputra gorge, which we had always intended to do. Wangdü hesitated and then said he'd have to ask his Chinese superior for permission. I reminded him that during our time in Lhasa, he had also been dependent on a superior—a Tibetan one. And now his superior was a Chinese.

Wangdü had been jailed by the Chinese during the Cultural Revolution, but now he had been so indoctrinated with Communist ideas that our conversation soon came to an end. As we separated, I told him that despite our differences of opinion we should still remain friends. To my relief, he agreed.

Since my visit a decade ago, more than 120,000 Tibetans have fled their country. They are now distributed in thirty-three countries all over the world.

When I came back to Europe in 1952, my first plan was to speak with Sven Hedin, with whom I had corresponded heavily while I was in Lhasa. He asked me to come see him in Stockholm, and it proved a wonderful meeting that lasted for two days. Even though he was well over eighty years old, lots of people were still coming to visit him for advice or his autograph. He showed me drawers that were arranged alphabetically, and under the letter "H" were all my letters from Lhasa as well as copies of most of what he had sent to me. This latter was wonderful to discover. As I was escaping from Lhasa in 1951, my load of precious *thangka*s and correspondence had fallen into the Kyichu River. The load had been saved, but the writing on the letters was blurred.

When I left Hedin, he gave me a complete set of his famous scientific work on southern Tibet. That autumn, when I was at a lecture in Austria, I read that he had died in Stockholm; on the same day I received a handwritten letter from him—the last letter he had written in his life. Sven Hedin had been my greatest living role model.

*Sven Hedin was an important role model for me. He had once tried to reach Lhasa himself, and was renowned for his knowledge of Tibet. He and I exchanged frequent letters while I was in Lhasa; he urged me to write down everything I saw.*

Peter Aufschnaiter stayed on in Lhasa when I left in 1951; he wanted to remain as long as he possibly could. Finally, after he heard that the Dalai Lama had fled, he too left Lhasa. He first headed for Kyirong, the "village of happiness," where we had spent much of 1945. There he found our old friend Ongdi, and in January 1952, the two of them left Tibet for Kathmandu. Aufschnaiter lived in Nepal for most of the rest of his life, working as an agricultural engineer first for Swiss Technical Aid, a development organization for poor countries, and then for the

Food and Agricultural Organization of the United Nations. Every three years he came on leave to Europe, where we went mountaineering together. He died in Innsbruck on October 12, 1973, at the age of seventy-three. He was the best partner I can imagine for such a grand adventure as we had together in Tibet.

The Dalai Lama's family continued to lead productive lives, always caring for their people. Norbu, the eldest son, was a carefree man when he was one of my closest friends in Lhasa. Before the Dalai Lama left Tibet in 1959, Norbu stayed with me in Austria for several months, as we wrote the book *Tibet Is My Country* together. We had to be very careful with our words, for the Dalai Lama was still in Lhasa, in the hands of the Chinese. Later, Norbu became a professor at Indiana University. Though a *rinpoche*, Norbu gave up his monk's robes to marry. Now retired, he acts as the Dalai Lama's representative in Tokyo.

Gyalyum Chemo, the Holy Mother of the Dalai Lama, escaped, too, in 1959. I saw her for the last time in Dharamsala not long before her death in 1962. Three of her grandchildren lived with her at her home, called the Kashmir Cottage. She was not only warmhearted, she was also very outspoken, as was evidenced when the Regent or others tried to stop my early visits with the young Dalai Lama; she had silenced them immediately with firm words, for which I am greatly in her debt.

My wonderful friend in Tibet, Lobsang Samten, died at the young age of fifty, in New Delhi. He and his wife Namlha (from the Tsarong family) had lived for a while in America after escaping from Tibet. But when they found their children started showing more interest in American than Tibetan culture, they moved back to Dharamsala, where they worked at the medical center.

The Dalai Lama's youngest brother, Ngari Rinpoche—born soon after our arrival in Lhasa—is the lovely boy on the cover of this book. As an incarnated lama, he inherited eight monasteries in Ladakh. He converted his mother's Kashmir Cottage into a little hotel, where he now lives.

During those unforgettable times we spent together in the Potala when he was a boy, the Dalai Lama and I read books and saw many films together. After viewing Shakespeare's *Henry V,* we discussed the powerful line, "Uneasy lies the head that wears the crown." I believe the young boy understood those words even then. I have often thought of this in subsequent years, because no other king in modern times has experienced its truth more than the Fourteenth Dalai Lama.

After the Seventeen-Point Agreement was reached between the Chinese and Tibetans, the Dalai Lama returned to Lhasa, where he spent most of the 1950s with his officers and noblemen. In 1956, three years before his final escape from the Chinese, I saw him for the first time in five years. He had obtained permission from the Chinese to visit Sikkim to attend the festivities celebrating the 2,500th anniversary of Buddha's birthday. The Dalai Lama was keen to see India and visit places connected with Mahatma Gandhi, a great role model of his. He also wanted to visit the tree under which the Buddha had received his enlightenment. When I heard of his visit to India, I rushed there by plane. We had a very short meeting, sandwiched between the ceremonies, and could exchange only a few words because of the presence of the Indian secret police.

Though many influential Tibetans and foreigners tried to convince His Holiness to stay in India, someone also told him, "Remember that in the mountains a tiger is a tiger; but a tiger who goes down to the plains becomes a dog." It was certainly one of the most difficult decisions the Dalai Lama had to make. Two of his brothers and I advised him to stay in India, but another brother and the state oracle advised the opposite. The Dalai Lama returned to Lhasa that year.

*Peter Aufschnaiter visiting me in Europe [top]. The Holy Family in Dharamsala: Gyalyum Chemo, Tsering Drölma, Thubten Norbu, Gyalu Thündup, Lobsang Samten, the Dalai Lama, Jetsün Pemala, Ngari Rinpoche.*

The Chinese did not adhere to the Seventeen-Point Agreement, and the situation in Tibet continued to deteriorate. In March 1959 a popular uprising took place. Tensions had been building, but the last straw to end Tibetan patience came when they suspected the Chinese planned to abduct the Dalai Lama. Disguised, His Holiness and his entourage departed Lhasa at night. The Chinese didn't discover his absence until he was already in the mountains of southern Tibet. For two weeks the group fled southward, reaching India on March 31.

With an assignment from *Life* magazine and the London *Daily Mail* to get the story of the escape, I went to India as these events took place. In the town of Tezpur the Dalai Lama spotted me in a crowd of people and instantly exclaimed: "*Dogpo! Dogpo!*" "Friend! Friend!" Later, in a special train, His Holiness was brought through India to the hill town of Dharamsala, where he and his group were interned by Prime Minister Nehru, an ally of China. Thus, almost exactly fifteen years after I had escaped from India and fled to Tibet, the Dalai Lama fled Tibet to come to India. Even though His Holiness was under a kind of house arrest, he quickly formed a government-in-exile.

His country, meanwhile, suffered greatly. Thousands died before the guns fell silent, and most of the males between sixteen and sixty were deported to China to do forced labor. Later, the ten-year-long Cultural Revolution led by the Red Guards caused even more havoc and devastation. Yet years of such brutal oppression did not shake the profound religious and cultural faith of the Tibetan people.

After the Cultural Revolution ended in the late 1970s, the Chinese government invited His Holiness to return to Tibet. Wary of this offer, the Dalai Lama sent an older brother, Lobsang Samten, and his younger sister, Jetsün Pemala, to see what had happened in Tibet. The Chinese had assumed that thirty years of indoctrination would have changed the Tibetans, perhaps made them passive. But the opposite happened: Thousands of excited citizens tore down the metal fences the Chinese had erected. Everyone wanted to see or touch the representatives of His Holiness. It was a heartbreaking demonstration of allegiance.

It is not the purpose of this book to detail what has happened to Tibet since I left. It is clear the Tibetans have maintained their reverence for the Dalai Lama just as admiration for him has grown widely in the rest of the world. Popular demand for Tibet's independence has been steadily increasing worldwide, a development that is mainly due to the endeavors and charisma of the Dalai Lama. Each year hundreds of thousands of people listen to his lectures and prayers, and many thousand more see exhibitions on Tibet and learn of the high standards of its old culture. Slowly the world has come to realize the extent to which Tibet's culture has been mutilated.

*The Dalai Lama at my home in Liechtenstein in 1991. When I was fifty, the Dalai Lama gave me a several-hundred-year-old bronze statue of Tshe Pame, the god of eternal life. Though it was meant only symbolically, now that I am eighty I feel it has fulfilled its promise of old age.*

The Dalai Lama and I see each other almost every year to remind people of the cause of Tibetan rights, to open an exhibition on Tibet, or just to have a visit. The boy I knew in Lhasa who was so curious about the outside world now travels everywhere. We've met in many countries; twice he has visited me and my family in our house in Liechtenstein, though more often I have gone to see him at his home-in-exile, the hill station of Dharamsala. This summer he will come to bless the opening of the Heinrich Harrer Museum in Hüttenberg, the town of my birth. Forty years ago in Lhasa I explained worldly things to him. Now I learn *from* him, especially about tolerance.

No doubt the greatest outside recognition for the Dalai Lama and his cause came when he won the 1989 Nobel Peace Prize. The citation says, "The Norwegian Nobel Committee has decided to award the 1989 Nobel Peace Price to the Fourteenth Dalai Lama, Tenzin Gyatso, the religious and political leader of the Tibetan people. The Committee wants to emphasize the fact that the Dalai Lama in his struggle for the liberation of Tibet consistently has opposed the use of violence. He has instead advocated peaceful solutions based upon tolerance and mutual respect, in order to preserve the historical and cultural heritage of his people."

It is not difficult to imagine my personal pride and gratitude in having one of the true great men of our time as a friend and as my lasting contact with the equally great nation that took me in when I was a penniless fugitive. That is why I have dedicated this book to the children of Tibet, that they may see these old pictures and read these stories and learn about how life used to be. My vision is that someday the people of Tibet, led by their Fourteenth Dalai Lama—the incarnation of Chenrezi, the God of Mercy and Compassion—will be happy again in a free Tibet.

# GLOSSARY

*Spelling a Tibetan word in the Latin alphabet is simply a phonetic approximation. Naturally, this process offers considerable variation in interpretation, especially when one considers the various European languages spoken by those doing the transliterations. The words below and in the text are spelled according to one accepted interpretation, but this system is neither more nor less valid than alternate spellings found in other texts.*

BARKOR—The inner circular path around the Tsuglagkhang in Lhasa. This is where the bazaar is located.

CHAGPORI—The "iron mountain"—*chag* means iron, and *ri* means mountain—atop which sat the medical school, now destroyed.

CHANG—Tibetan beer, made from fermented barley, wheat, rice, or millet.

CHANGTHANG—The high plateau in central Tibet where the nomads lived and where we crossed on our journey from India to Lhasa.

CHENPO—Used in high titles, meaning "big" or "great."

CHÖRTEN—A tomb, or memorial used in the Buddhist world. Known as a *stupa* in Sanskrit.

DALAI LAMA—The Mongolian name (meaning "great ocean") for the spiritual and secular ruler of Tibet, who is considered an incarnation of Chenrezi, the god of mercy and compassion. Inside Tibet, he is known as Gyalpo Rinpoche, Kundün, or Jishi Norbu.

DAMARU—A drum that is twirled back-and-forth to swing mallets that strike the drum; used for religious purposes.

DHARAMSALA—The hill village in the Himalchal Pradesh of northern India, where the Tibetan government-in-exile resides, as does the Fourteenth Dalai Lama.

DOB-DOB—The fierce-looking monk-police from Drepung Monastery who were also renowned for their athletics.

DREPUNG—This was the largest monastery in the world, five miles west of Lhasa. Literally, *drepung* means "rice heap." It was one of the "three pillars" of the Tibetan government, along with Sera and Ganden.

DZONG—Fort.

GANDEN—This was the third largest monastery in Tibet, thirty-five miles east of Lhasa. One of the former "three pillars" of the Tibetan government, along with Sera and Drepung.

GESHE—A degree monks receive after going through all their examinations—like a "Doctor of Divinity." (Unlike a *rinpoche*, a *geshe* is not incarnate.)

GONPA—A Tibetan Buddhist monastery.

GYALYAB CHEMO—The Dalai Lama's father.

GYALYUM CHEMO—The Dalai Lama's mother.

GYANGTSE—A town with a large fortress, located at a junction of large caravan routes. Formerly the seat of the Indian Trade Mission.

HENRIG—What the Tibetans called me because they have no "ei" or "k" sounds, as pronouncing my name in German would call for.

HIS HOLINESS—Honorific expression for the Dalai Lama.

HOLY FAMILY, HOLY MOTHER—Honorific terms for the Dalai Lama's family and mother.

JIGME—The boy whom I rescued from drowning. This was a popular name meaning "without fear."

JOKHANG—The room in the Tsuglagkhang that held the statue of Jowo Rinpoche. People would say, "I'm going to the Jokhang," even if they were actually going to the Tsuglagkhang without entering the Jokhang itself.

KHANG—House or temple.

KHATAG—A good-luck scarf used for special occasions like welcoming visitors, birthdays, marriages, farewells, and certain religious ceremonies.

KHENPO—An abbot, or a university president in a monastery.

KOR—A ring road, or circular path, often around a holy site.

KYICHU—The holy river that flowed past Lhasa. This is the river on which I built the dike to protect the Norbulingkha from flooding.

KYIRONG—The "village of happiness" where Peter Aufschnaiter and I stayed nine months during our journey from India to Lhasa.

LADAKH—A province of Kashmir, in India, on the western border of Tibet. It has extensive Tibetan culture, including about 100 monasteries.

LAMA—A spiritual teacher in Tibetan Buddhism, known as a guru in Sanskrit; usually a monk, but a layman could also be considered a "lama."

LINGKHA—A garden, or park.

LINGKOR—The five-mile holy circular path around Lhasa, the Potala, and Chagpori.

LOBSANG—A popular Tibetan name. Lobsang Samten was the Dalai Lama's third-oldest brother and one of my best friends in Lhasa.

MÖNLAM—A religious prayer.

MÖNLAM CHENPO—The "great prayer" following New Year.

NGARI RINPOCHE—The Dalai Lama's youngest brother.

NORBU—A popular Tibetan name meaning "jewel." Thubten Jigme Norbu is the Dalai Lama's eldest brother.

NORBULINGKHA—The Dalai Lama's summer palace, the "jewel garden."

NYIMA—My servant in Lhasa. The name means "sun."

POTALA—The Dalai Lama's winter palace. Thirteen stories tall, this is where many government functions and ceremonies were held. Tibetans called it simply "tse," meaning "summit."

RANK—The Tibetan government, called the depashung, was divided into seven ranks as follows. First—the Dalai Lama. Second—the regent, or the prime minister when the Dalai Lama is a minor. Third—the four cabinet ministers—three lay and one monk. Fourth—four chief secretaries from the Tsedrung elite, four financial secretaries from the lay nobility, and governors of the large districts. Fifth—nearly 100 treasury officers, judges, and other functionaries; Peter Aufschnaiter and I were in this rank. Sixth and Seventh—clerks, inspectors, accountants, etc.

RIMSHI—The fourth rank.

RINPOCHE—The term used to address an incarnate lama; means "precious one."

SERA—The second largest monastery in Tibet, two miles north of Lhasa. One of the former "three pillars" of the Tibetan government, along with Ganden and Drepung.

SHIGATSE—The capital of the western province of Tsang.

SHÖ—The village at the foot of the Potala. The military was garrisoned here, and the prison was located here too.

THANGKA—A scroll painting, usually about holy subjects. The large ones are embroidered.

TIBET—This word was hardly known in Tibet itself. Internally, they mostly used the name "Bhö." Only during the twentieth century has the name "Tibet" come into use within its own borders.

TORMA—A conical sacred offering in ceremonies.

TSAMPA—Parched barley flour, the Tibetan's staple food.

TSANGPO—The Tibetan name for the Brahmaputra River.

TSARONG—A famous Tibetan family in Lhasa. Tsarong Sawang Chenpo was my host during my first two years in Lhasa. His son Dadul Namgyel Tsarong, better known as George, became one of my best friends.

TSE—Summit.

TSEDRÖN—Fifteen members of the Tsedrung who held the higher rank of "Drönyer." Their senior was called "Drönyer Chemo."

TSEDRUNG—The elite group of 175 monks who made up the "ecclesiastical court" that met in the Potala every morning.

TSUGLAGKHANG—The inner temple in Lhasa, located in the Barkor; it was built in the seventh century and is often referred to as Jokhang—"Jowo" was the statue of Jowo Rinpoche inside, and "khang" means house.

WANGDÜ—A popular Tibetan name. Shokhang Wangdü Tsedrung was one of my best friends in Lhasa.

YAPSHI—A house belonging to a family into which a Dalai Lama has been born.

# NOTES ON THE PICTURES

*The following notes will identify some of the individuals whom I knew best during my years in Lhasa. The process of spelling Tibetan words and names in the Latin alphabet is at best making a phonetic approximation. Therefore, do not be surprised if I have identified someone here or elsewhere in the text with a spelling that differs from other published texts. Also, the nobility often have several names that might be used under different circumstances, and not all of which I will necessarily list each time I reference that person. I hope this does not create too much confusion.*

p. 54: Departing are Hugh Edward Richardson's servants.

p. 55: The woman is Surkhang Lhacham Kusho, the wife of Surkhang Sawang Chemo, the senior lay cabinet minister; her visiting relative is Yüthok Sey.

p. 57: At far right is Kunsangtse Depön; in the middle are two finance ministers who had visited the U.S.A.; at right is Surkhang Depön.

p. 60: At far left is one of the Holy Family's servants; in the lower left is Tsering Drölma's son.

p. 61: This front wall is the servants' quarters; the Holy Family lived in another building within the courtyard.

p. 63: Lower: The woman on the left in fancy clothing is Tsering Drölma; in front of her is her husband, holding Pemala Jetsün's hand; at far right is their son; behind are servants.

p. 75: The tallest peak in the background—immediately behind the Potala—is Gephe Utse.

p. 76: Upper: The tallest person on the left is Jigme Surkhang; next to him is Shokhang Sey (Wangdü Tsedrung's younger brother); the others are servants.

p. 77: The cabinet minister on the far left is Ragashar Sawang Chenpo; the one between the two umbrellas on the right is Rampa Sawang Chenpo; the men in the wide-brimmed hats bearing the umbrellas are servants.

p. 78: The mountain in the background is Gephe Utse.

p. 81: Clockwise from the left are Tsipön Lukhang, Rampa Shöpa, Rimshi Pemba, and Pagasha Magoki.

p. 82: On the far right is Wangdü.

p. 83: The woman looking most directly at the camera is Surkhang Lhacham; the woman on the far right is her sister.

p. 84: Myself.

p. 85: On the left is Wangdü; in the middle is Lobsang Samten.

p. 86: That's me about to serve.

p. 87: Top: On the left is Lobsang; on the right is Khenchung. Bottom: On the left is Phala Drönyer Chemo.

p. 91: Left to right: Wangdü, Kunsangtse, me.

p. 93: Phala Drönyer Chemo.

p. 97: On the left, wearing the leather strap used to carry the boat, is Surkhang Wangchuk; inside the boat is Wangdü; looking into the boat is Kunsangtse Sey.

p. 100: On the left is Dadul Namgyel Tsarong (George); next to him is Samdrub; the monk is Shälngo Shingnyer.

p. 103: George is on horseback.

p. 104: Above: George is seated, flanked by six adjutants; behind him are the two servants who were leading his horse on page 103. Below: George is on the left; Samdrub on the right; between them is a *tsampa* bowl.

p. 106: Phala Drönyer Chemo's younger brother.

p. 107: On the far left is Agu Thönpa, a famous singer.

p. 116: The woman in the doorway is Yüthog Lhacham Kusho, the elder sister of minister Surkhang. On the far right is Surkhang Wangchuk, the governor of Gyangtse.

p. 117: Minister Surkhang's daughter.

p. 150: The structure in the background is a monument for a past smallpox epidemic.

p. 163: The building on the right is the house of Liushar Dzasa, the monk foreign minister.

p. 171: The small *thangka* was also carried in the procession between the Norbulingkha and the Potala.

p. 173: The State Oracle, Nechung, in front of the Tsuglagkhang.

p. 188: The man walking on the right is my servant, Nyima.

p. 202: The man on the far right is Sholkhang Sey, the governor of Phari; in front of him are officers of the caravan retinue.

# INDEX

The photographic section of this book is organized by subject, each with its own title. Those titles are listed below in bold type.

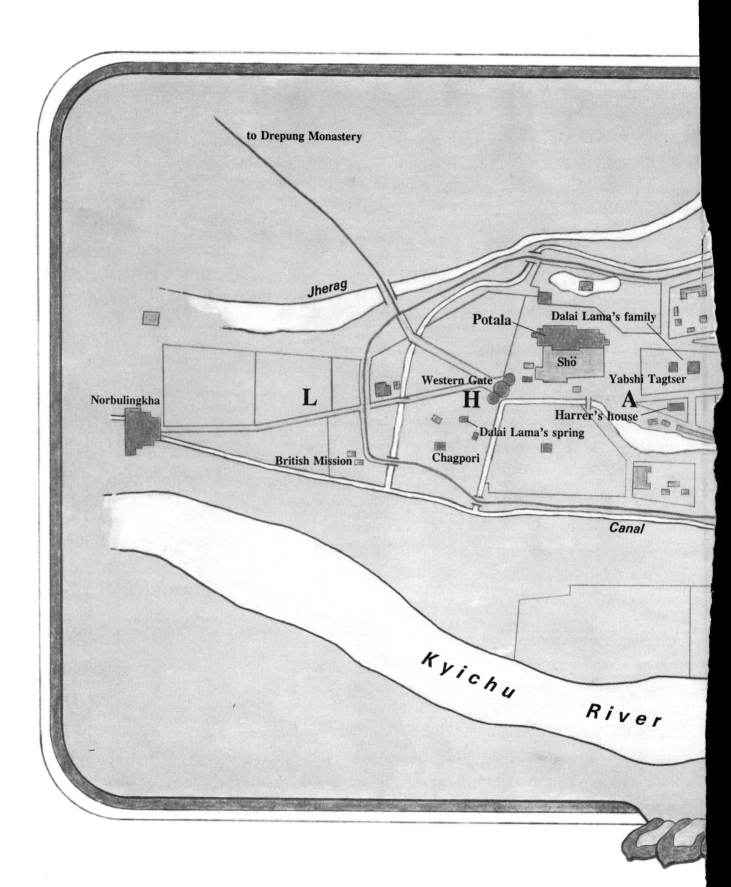

to Drepung Monastery

Jherag

Potala

Dalai Lama's family

Shö

Western Gate

Yabshi Tagtser

**L**

**H**

**A**

Norbulingkha

Harrer's house

Dalai Lama's spring

British Mission

Chagpori

Canal

K y i c h u    R i v e r

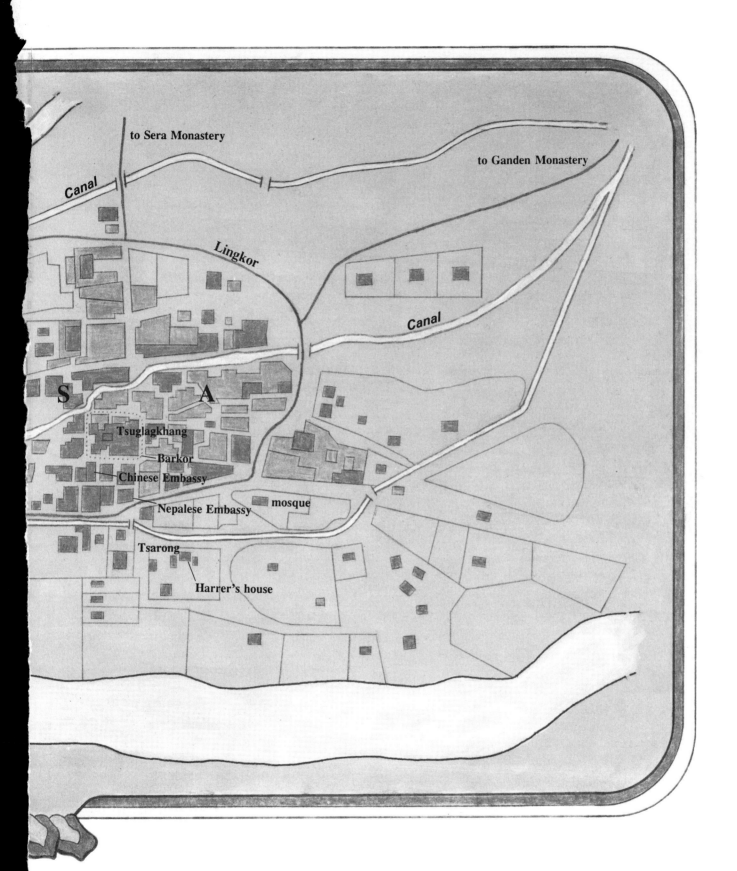

# LOST LHASA
## Heinrich Harrer's Tibet

Heinrich Harrer and the Dalai Lama in Washington, D.C., 1991.
*Photograph by Alois Anwander*

Innocent of the rest of the world, Tibetan civilization developed over the centuries with unparalleled purity and verve. It was a brilliant, joyous, inspired culture whose sciences, arts, and even politics flowed from spiritual beliefs and practices. That culture was shattered suddenly and forever in 1950, when the Chinese invaded Tibet.

At the time, Austrian mountaineer Heinrich Harrer had been in Tibet for seven years. As he fled, he brought with him negatives of the pictures he had been taking with left-behind film and borrowed cameras, pictures documenting life in Lhasa, candid images of the people who had made him almost one of their own. His *Seven Years in Tibet*, which has sold over three million copies since its publication in 1953, is illustrated with only a few of these photographs.

*Lost Lhasa* presents 200 of Harrer's extraordinary images, capturing a luminous, exotic world. With an intimacy and understanding that only Heinrich Harrer could impart, the photographs give us a last glimpse of life in and around Lhasa, Tibet's capital city and the locus to which all Tibet gravitated.

Energized by Harrer's detail-rich commentary, these pages are a powerful and moving resurrection of life in Lhasa—from Buddhist ceremonies to family celebrations, from outings in the countryside to men's and women's games of chance, from spirited athletic contests to the sad flight of Harrer's avid pupil, the eighteen-year-old Dalai Lama.

Photographer/mountaineer Galen Rowell's introduction gives a shining perspective to Harrer's achievement and helps make this important book, in Harrer's words, "the culmination of my half century of involvement with Tibet."

*200 black-and-white illustrations*

Heinrich Harrer (b. 1912) is one of the great explorers of the twentieth century. The first climber to scale the sheer north face of Europe's notorious Eiger, the intrepid Austrian set out for the Himalayas before he was thirty years old. He reached Lhasa only after escaping from a British internment camp in India during World War II and spending two harrowing years on foot in the Tibetan highlands. Once accepted by the Tibetans, Harrer became an official in the Lhasa government, befriending the young Fourteenth Dalai Lama and tutoring him until the Chinese invasion of Tibet at the end of 1950. Honored by virtually all the world's great exploration and mountaineering societies, Harrer lives today in Liechtenstein with his wife Carina.

*Front cover:* The young Ngari Rinpoche, the Dalai Lama's youngest brother, with the Potala in the background. *Back cover:* Lhasans on makeshift ice skates on the frozen Kyichu River below Chagpori hill. *Photographs by Heinrich Harrer*

Harry N. Abrams, Inc.
100 Fifth Avenue
New York, N.Y. 10011
www.abramsbooks.com